EBURY PRESS
RECIPES FOR LIFE

Sudha Menon is the author of five non-fiction books, including *Legacy, Gifted* and *Devi, Diva or She-Devil*. She is the founder of the popular Get Writing and Writing With Women workshops series and a motivational speaker. She is also a model, and a diversity and inclusion ambassador.

ADVANCE PRAISE FOR THE BOOK

'As a professional chef, I draw inspiration from my mother's recipes every day and base my own cooking on what I grew up eating. Knowingly or unknowingly, our mothers' cooking, including its familiarity, comfort and methods, becomes a reference point as we start our own culinary journeys. A book like this is the best gift to our families—and indeed to ourselves—as it not only documents the recipes, the methods and the ingredients of our favourite dishes but also preserves associated memories, thereby allowing us to relive precious moments in our lives.'
—Naren Thimmaiah, executive chef, Vivanta, Bengaluru

'With this book, Sudha Menon brings to the fore a very important aspect of our lives, our heritage through food. In spite of being the most documented (think phone cameras) generation till date, we have lost touch with what makes us who we are. This book addresses that missing link. Read it, you won't regret it.'—Parvana Boga Noorani, author and food writer

'What is so unique about the food cooked by our mothers? Do we love her food because she is the world's best cook? That may not be true but the food our moms cook for us is like a warm hug. When we go away from home, live alone and feel homesick, we think of "*maa ke hath ka khana*". Sudha's book brings out the delicious stories of mothers and the food they cook, and the stories are narrated most delightfully.'—Sadaf Hussain, chef and author

'The stories that make up this book are a much-needed salve of warmth in an increasingly fragmented life. This is an invaluable documentation of day-to-day life in India. The recipes can add oodles of joy to your kitchen.'—Kalyan Karmakar, author of *Travelling Belly*, and food blogger

'What I love about this book is that it shows the unity and diversity of Indian food. More importantly, it highlights the fact that in a world and at a time where family bonds are becoming more and more strained with distance and children growing up in different cultures, it is clear that food is often the glue that keeps these bonds alive.'—Karen Anand, author and food entrepreneur

RECIPES
for LIFE

WELL-KNOWN PERSONALITIES
REVEAL STORIES, MEMORIES
and AGE-OLD FAMILY RECIPES

Foreword by VIKAS KHANNA

SUDHA
MENON

EBURY
PRESS

An imprint of Penguin Random House

EBURY PRESS

USA | Canada | UK | Ireland | Australia
New Zealand | India | South Africa | China

Ebury Press is part of the Penguin Random House group of companies
whose addresses can be found at global.penguinrandomhouse.com

Published by Penguin Random House India Pvt. Ltd
4th Floor, Capital Tower 1, MG Road,
Gurugram 122 002, Haryana, India

First published in Ebury Press by Penguin Random House India 2021

ISBN 9780143452577

Typeset in Sabon by Manipal Technologies Limited, Manipal
Printed at Manipal Technologies Limited, Manipal

www.penguin.co.in

To my mother, Pramila Radhakrishnan, who raised me with an abundance of love and the tastiest morsels ever.

'You can prepare the tastiest meal with just water, salt, a couple of onions and some chillies. The most important ingredient in food is the love you cook it with,' you always say, Amma, and I know now that it is true.

CONTENTS

viii   CONTENTS

AUTHOR'S NOTE

Sitting in a corner of the spice shelf in my kitchen is a bottle with 'aai's khichadi masala' written on it in her familiar, now fading, handwriting.

Aai, my mother-in-law, handed it over to me one winter afternoon when I visited her, and I still remember what she said: 'Prashant la moogachi khichadi karoon de. Tyala khoop avadte [Prepare moong khichadi for Prashant with this masala. He loves it].'

Aai passed away a few months after that from the ravages of dementia. When I opened the bottle a couple of months ago, the masala was as aromatic as it was all those years ago, but I could not bring myself to use it for fear it would get over and with it would go the last memory of her. One of my biggest regrets is that neither I, nor anyone else in the family, ever wrote down any of her recipes because we simply presumed she would always be around to feed us with love. And now, her culinary legacy is gone with her, lost forever.

Over the last few years, my sisters and I have been discussing taking down Amma's recipes so that her grandchildren and those who come after them are able to enjoy the legacy she leaves behind. We worry that it is already too late because Amma's memory is not the same any more.

While her anecdotes about family recipes learnt under the loving supervision of her trio of aunts in Kerala and from her mother-in-law were razor sharp just four years ago, she now struggles to remember the ingredients and methods of preparing her favourite dishes with which she pampered us.

I have heard this story countless times from friends and acquaintances—stories of women from Amma's generation, fabulous, talented cooks who passed on and could not leave their culinary legacy behind. I decided then that I would put this book together so that we could capture much-loved family recipes and enjoy cooking the dishes in our kitchens.

As a teenager, I remember refusing to enter the kitchen to learn even the rudiments of cooking. It was only when I became a young mother that I started my own journey of cooking. But now, when my daughter, a talented pastry chef, comes visiting, I enjoy spending time with her, cooking up a couple of Amma's dishes. There is a special magic that happens over the comfort of a shared meal, garnished with laughter and endless love.

This book is a celebration of the bonds that we forge with our mothers and those who cook with love for us. It is for a reason that we say that 'maa ke haath ka khaana' is the best meal in the world and a recipe for life.

Sudha Menon
July 2021

FOREWORD

The true meaning of culture is based on the rituals of continuity. From small traditions and ceremonies to big festivals, culture binds us all. It gives the nation a shared identity.

For me, India's true fabric lies in these traditions. Growing up in a middle-class family in Amritsar, I was surrounded by them every day for almost thirty years. When I moved to the US in 2000, I started missing these traditions and realized their importance. This holds true especially now when we are all dispersing in our quest for individuality.

In many homes, the kitchen is the temple of stability and togetherness. The food that gets cooked there and the recipes are part of our identity.

In a country where generations of mothers have passed down age-old family recipes to their daughters, daughters-in-law and, indeed, to their sons by word of mouth, this book was waiting to be written.

I have always said this: We love and cherish the food that our mothers raised us with. No matter where we travel to or how many sophisticated restaurants around the world we dine at, we always want to come home to the food we grew up eating.

As a little boy, growing up in Amritsar, I watched my mother cooking in the kitchen along with my biji (grandmother), both of them working in tandem. They bonded over pots of bubbling curries and the sizzle of tempering, each recounting stories of food from their respective homes.

I was fascinated watching them at work. In fact, it was from Biji and her anecdotes about food from her maternal home that I first developed an interest in cooking, little knowing that this would lay the foundation for a career in the culinary world.

I have worked with some of the world's best chefs, brilliant men and women who conjure up a mind-boggling variety of food, skilfully measuring ingredients and following well-documented recipes to a T. Over the decades, I have been amazed how Indian kitchens and culinary traditions have survived and thrived on just instructions passed on from mothers to daughters or other younger women of the household. In some cases, sons too have learnt cooking from their mothers because of their passion for food, but what is striking is the almost complete absence of documenting of the recipes. I know very few families where recipes of the food cooked at home are written down and followed. A pinch of this, a hint of that, a sprinkle of the other and a handful of love seems to be their way of cooking.

This book is significant and special because it sets out to document for posterity the recipes of our mothers and grandmothers, all of whom are versatile, talented, passionate cooks and have nurtured their families with food made with love for decades. We make the mistake of presuming that our mothers will always be around to cook for us, so we never even bother to find out what goes into the making of the salans, subzis, biryanis and sweetmeats. Until it is too late, and the nurturer has left for her onward journey.

In an age where the old, extended joint families of yore have gone and we live in tiny nuclear families where children know almost nothing about their grandparents, this book will help our children know about them, their lives and the food traditions that have stayed in the family.

This is a precious book and a must read for both young and old. This book will build bridges between the past, the present and the future. Gift it to the food lovers in your family! I urge all of you to take inspiration from this book and start documenting your own family recipes from your mothers, mothers-in-law and those who conjure up soul food in your kitchen every day.

Bon Appetit!

Vikas Khanna
Michelin-starred chef, author, filmmaker, humanitarian
New York City
November 2020

AJIT AGARKAR, CRICKETER, COMMENTATOR

MOTHER: MEENA AGARKAR

As a little boy, I was a poor eater, and I think both Aai (mom) and Ajji (grandmother) really struggled to make sure I had enough food in my tummy. Their challenge doubled when I started playing cricket at the age of ten, because they had to make sure what I ate was nourishing enough to give me the stamina to follow my dream of playing for my country someday.

Since Aai was a working woman, lunch was always at Ajji's house in Dadar. That was also where I first started developing an interest in cricket. We lived in Worli, and I remember Aai would pick me up after work. She would get into the kitchen right after we got home, so that she could cook dinner.

As a child, I refused to eat most vegetables, but I could eat bhindi and gawar (cluster beans) every single day if I was allowed, because Aai made delicious bhajis out of these. What I also remember from those days was that we ate simple food at home because Aai was working. By the time I was twelve, I had no time to think of fancy food or treats because I was completely immersed in cricket.

1

Even so, I had certain favourites that Aai cooked, such as her delicious pohe and sabudana khichadi. These were usually Sunday treats because weekday mornings were rushed—my parents had to go to work and my sister and I had to get ready for school. As my involvement in cricket increased, I started going to the training ground straight from school, reaching home only in time for dinner.

Unlike other homes, we did not have grand Sunday lunches or dinners because Aai would be exhausted from the pace of the weekdays, but she always made sure our dinners were tasty. I loved dinner time because that was when we would all be together as a family. We chatted about our day and relaxed over the food.

I started travelling for cricket when I was still in my teens, and over the last two decades, I have travelled all over the world, playing cricket for my country. It was a bit of a challenge in the initial months because I am from a vegetarian family, but I soon discovered the variety of non-vegetarian options available and started enjoying them.

I remember Aai once told me that since I needed to build up my stamina, she was okay with learning to cook non-vegetarian food at home. It touched me immensely, but I told her I was fine with eating her tasty vegetarian food at home.

Even today, nothing compares to the taste of a simple meal of varan-bhaat (Maharashtrian style dal and chawal) that she served with an accompaniment of coriander chutney. She also made a spicy dry chutney with roasted khobra (dry coconut) and til, a Maharashtrian staple that I particularly missed during my long overseas tours.

Both Aai and Ajji made terrific phodnichi poli, a dish made of leftover chapattis, seasoned with cumin and mustard, and tossed in a fiery masala of fried onions, chillies and coriander leaves. Ajji often served it when I came back home from school because she knew I loved it and would not fuss about eating it.

As a kid I had a sweet tooth and I could have any number of Aai's puran polis—she made the softest puran polis stuffed with jaggery and served them with a tiny dollop of home-made ghee. These were a regular on our dinner table because all of us loved them. Even today when I visit Aai, I call in advance so that she can ready this meal for me. And when I return home, she packs some for my son, Raj, who loves puran polis too. Mango season even today means Aai's polis with aam ras that all of us love to feast on.

Our family has a 125-year-old tradition of installing Lord Ganesha on Ganesh Chaturthi. When I was growing up, on the day of his arrival, the ladies of the house would get busy preparing an array of dishes that would go into the naivedya, the edibles offered to the lord. As a little boy, I looked forward to this meal for the goodies in it, including dalimbichi usal (field beans cooked with goda masala, coconut and other spices), lal bhoplyache puri (sweet puris made from red pumpkin and jaggery), bhajaniche wade (a fried savoury made with aromatic multigrain flour and a variety of spices), varan-bhaat and Aai's signature green chutney.

Aai's modaks were always special, but the day we welcomed Ganpati into our home, it seemed like they became extra special—the jaggery and coconut filling inside would be gooey and delicious and the rice flour wrapping would melt in the mouth. And as for the varan-bhaat on the naivedya plate, I would wait for it to be offered to the lord before it was given to me. I would then pour home-made ghee on the mound of varan-bhaat and dig into it happily. There would be green chutney on the side and dalimbi usal added to the grand

Konkanastha Brahmin feast that Aai, Ajji and Attya (paternal aunt) would prepare for the naivedya.

During Diwali, Aai's pharal (special snacks and sweetmeats) was the highlight of our celebrations. Despite her busy schedule, she would go all out to pamper us with lots of goodies. My favourite was her spicy chiwda with a profusion of fried khobra and peanuts that gave it a delightful crunch. Next was her bhajanichi chakli that was crisp and yet melted in the mouth when you bit into it.

Over the last few decades, I have developed a taste for non-vegetarian food, which I eat wherever I go in the world. But when I return to India, I head home to Aai for the best vegetarian food.

CRISPY DRY COCONUT
AND SESAME SEED CHUTNEY

Ingredients

- 1 cup grated dry coconut
- 1/4 cup sesame seeds
- 1 tbs oil
- 1/4 tsp each mustard seeds, cumin seeds, asafoetida and powdered sugar
- 1/2 tsp red chilli powder
- Salt to taste

Method

- Roast grated khobra on a low flame.
- Dry roast the sesame seeds separately. Remove and keep aside.

- In another pan, heat oil and add mustard and cumin seeds. Let them splutter. Add asafoetida, turmeric and chilli powder and switch off the gas so that the spices don't burn. Add powdered sugar, salt to taste, the roasted khobra and sesame seeds.
- Mix well.
- This chutney can be had as an accompaniment to rice and dal or rotis and vegetables. Always adds a spicy kick to the meal.

GAWARICHI BHAJI WITH GODA MASALA

Ingredients

- 1/2 kg cluster beans cleaned and cut into small pieces
- 1/4 kg red pumpkin cut into cubes
- 1 tbs oil
- 1/4 tsp mustard and cumin seeds each
- 1/4 tsp asafoetida and turmeric powder each
- 1/2 tsp chilli powder
- 1 tsp goda masala (found in most stores)
- 1 tbs jaggery
- 1 tbs roasted peanuts, crushed or ground coarsely.
- Salt to taste
- Grated fresh coconut and coriander for garnishing

Method

- Heat oil in a pan and add mustard and cumin seeds. Let them splutter.
- Add asafoetida and turmeric powder.

- Add cut beans and pumpkin cubes. Sauté for a couple of minutes.
- Add chilli powder, goda masala and a little water.
- Stir, cover and cook till the beans are tender.
- Add roasted and crushed groundnuts, jaggery and salt.
- Stir and cook for another five minutes.
- Remove in serving bowl and garnish with freshly grated coconut and finely chopped coriander.
- This is a Konkanastha Brahmin favourite and is great with both hot chapattis and rice.

CHIWDA

Ingredients

- 500 gm rice flakes (poha) of the thin variety. The thicker variety of the same rice flakes is used to make another Maharashtrian staple, pohe.
- 100 gm groundnut
- 100 gm roasted Bengal gram
- 50 gm dry coconut cut into thin slices
- 1/2 tsp each mustard, cumin and sesame seeds
- 1/2 tsp asafoetida and turmeric powder
- 1 tsp amchur powder
- 1 tsp powdered sugar
- 4 chillies cut into pieces and a few curry leaves
- Salt to taste
- Oil as per preference

Method

- First rub oil lightly into the rice flakes and keep aside for an hour.

- In a thick bottomed pan, roast the flakes on low heat until they turn crisp.
- Keep aside.
- Take some oil in the pan and fry the peanuts till crisp. Keep aside.
- Now fry the khobra slices lightly, keep aside.
- Then fry the roasted Bengal gram lightly and keep aside.
- Heat 2 to 3 tbs oil in the pan, add mustard, cumin and sesame seeds. Let them splutter.
- Add curry leaves and chopped chillies.
- Switch off the gas.
- Add asafoetida, turmeric, powdered sugar, amchur powder and salt.
- Finally, add the roasted rice flakes, peanuts, khobra slices and roasted Bengal gram. Mix well.
- Store in an airtight container after it has cooled down.
- This is an important part of the Diwali pharal tradition in Maharashtrian homes. Nowadays, it is made throughout the year as a teatime snack since it is fairly nutritious and a good substitute for fried snacks.

AMISH TRIPATHI, AUTHOR

MOTHER: USHA TRIPATHI

Sunday lunches at our home in Kansbahal, a small town in Orissa, where Papa worked for L&T, is my earliest memory of Ma's cooking. Ours was a family of modest means, and Ma had to be careful with the limited money she had at her disposal. Therefore, the food she put on the table was simple but always delicious.

Sunday lunch was special because of the puris and slightly more luxurious accompaniments like paneer or kaddu ki subzi, which we could not afford daily. What made the meal more special was that we—my parents, three siblings and I—would eat together as a family.

Ma made the best kaddu ki subzi and puri. I also loved her rice khichdi, warm and gooey, which she served with ghee, dahi, papad and a sprinkle of buknu masala. I have never tasted anything as distinctive as buknu masala in any other part of India, and I remember how a mere sprinkle of it would immediately enhance the taste of even the most insipid dish. The buknu masala was Ma's favourite travel staple and would go on rotis, parathas or whatever food we were carrying along with us.

Ma is from Gwalior in MP and my father is from Varanasi in UP, but the food we ate was largely simple fare from the Purvanchal region of UP where meals begin with roti and end with rice. Our daily meals were largely vegetarian, comprising dal, roti, chawal and subzi. Although my parents enjoyed fish, they preferred to eat it at restaurants.

My strongest memory of Ma and food will always be her golden rule that we had to eat whatever was cooked for the family, because it was 'good' for us. I will never forget how Didi and I got into trouble once, because we pushed away our thalis when we saw karela subzi on them. Ma was so furious that she made us eat karela for lunch and dinner for the entire week. I was upset back then, but I understand her better now. She would say that if we got used to having things our way right from childhood, we would not be able to handle life's ups and downs when we grew up. 'Learn to make do with whatever you have,' she would say. I am glad we got those lessons early on, because now I am able to handle tough situations when they come.

Festivals and festivities were a huge part of our growing-up years. I remember how Mahashivratri was a big occasion at home, with prayers, puja and prasad. Festive meals were super special because everything was cooked in pure ghee, which was a luxury in those days. Ma brought out her stock of basmati rice on these occasions to make delicious pulao. Festivals also meant we got to enjoy three to four subzis instead of one. Kheer was a staple at these meals.

I have always had a sweet tooth and sometimes crave Ma's delicious besan ladoos and her hand-churned shrikhand, a dish that involved an elaborate two-day process. Since she believed in healthy and nutritious eating, we kids were rarely allowed to eat store-bought snacks. Instead, she made sweet and savoury varieties of mathri for us to snack on when we returned from school or from the playground.

Unlike Papa, Ma was never the pampering kind. She told me much later that she read in the *Chanakya Neeti* that parents should envelop their kids in love till they are around five years old so that they are stable and secure; be tough with them between the ages of five and sixteen so that they learn to be disciplined and committed to hard work; and from the age of seventeen, parents should become their friends. Ma did exactly that.

I remember when I was in boarding school, she would write me long letters about life, philosophy and how to lead a fulfilled life. She would write about the importance of good education, determination, commitment to excellence and integrity. Ma is the very foundation of who I am and what I have achieved in life.

Despite being the tougher parent, Ma was incredibly generous, especially towards her children. Milk was expensive for us back then and so was butter, but she made sure all four of us got a glass of milk every morning before going to school. She controlled how much butter we got to eat, insisting it was 'not good' for us.

Later in life, Ma made friends with the wife of one of Papa's colleagues and learnt to make baked aubergines from her. Ma's Indianized version of the dish became a family favourite, and I looked forward to being treated to it every birthday. Ma is seventy-nine now and although she loves cooking even today, she ventures into the kitchen only on rare occasions. When my nephew visited from the UK, she made kaddu ki subzi, puri and baked aubergine for him, and all of it disappeared from the table in the blink of an eye.

MA'S KADDU KI SUBZI

Ma insists that this subzi is power packed with nutrition because pumpkins are rich in vitamins.

Ingredients

- 500 gm red pumpkin cubed, with tender skin intact
- Lemon-sized ball of tamarind soaked in warm water and pulp extracted
- 3 tsp mustard oil for cooking
- Red chilli powder, methi and mustard seeds, and haldi for seasoning and as per preference
- Half a tsp of jaggery or as per preference

Method

- Heat the oil in a pan and splutter the methi and mustard seeds.
- Add the turmeric and red chilli powder and quickly add the cubed pumpkins.
- Sauté for 5–6 minutes, cover and cook for a few minutes.
- This subzi needs no water as the pumpkin must cook in its own juice.
- Uncover when more than half cooked, add salt and jaggery, and mix well. Now add the pulp of the tamarind and cook for another 5 mins, mixing well.
- This sweet-sour subzi is delicious with puris.

PANYUCHA

This is an unusual traditional urad dal recipe that is served to baraatis during weddings and is both delicious and nutritious.

Ingredients

* 1 cup (small bowl) urad dal, washed and soaked for around 2 hours
* 2 cloves
* 2 pieces of badi elaichi and chhoti elaichi
* 3 to 5 black peppercorns
* A small piece of dalchini
* 1 tej patta
* Haldi, salt, red chilli powder and dhania powder as per preference
* 1-inch piece of ginger

Method

* Grind the soaked urad dal to a fine paste with salt and ginger and tie it up tightly in a piece of cloth.
* In a large pan, boil about 2 litres of water and when it is boiling well add the urad dal paste tied up in the cloth.
* Continue to boil till the urad dal bag rises to the top and floats. The urad dal will be hard when you touch it. Put off the gas and leave the bag in the water.
* Take a few spoons of water and to this add red chilli powder, haldi, coriander powder and garam masala. Mix them well into a paste.
* In a hot pan, add 2 to 3 teaspoons of mustard oil or ghee and splutter the whole spices.
* When the spices have spluttered, add the paste of the powdered spices and mix well.
* Add adequate quantity of boiling water from the urad dal pan into the seasoning. Continue boiling the water.

- Simultaneously, take out the urad dal cake from the bag and cut it into barfi-shaped pieces and add to the boiling water.
- When ready, the Panyucha will have slightly thickish consistency like the gravy of aloo tamatar subzi.
- Serve with steaming hot rice and papad.

ANAVILA MISRA, DESIGNER

MOTHER: URMIL SINDHU

The highlight of my childhood will always, always be the family's winter visit to my paternal grandmother's (dadiji's) house in Hashupur, a tiny village in Uttar Pradesh.

Dadiji had lived in the village alone for a long time because she lost her husband, my dadaji, very early. His sudden death made her a working woman who had to take care of her farm and animals, and she soon came to be not very fond of spending time in the kitchen. Sometimes just a pail of milk, right after the cow was milked, was her meal, and she would be happy and content.

She looked forward to our visit, and as soon as we reached, she would settle Papa down and then set off with me in tow, to find the best saag in the village. Such was the simplicity of life in the village that she would visit various families, telling them that her son was visiting and she wanted the freshest greens to make his favourite sarson ka saag. And such was the generosity of the families that we would often return home with a bagful of saag, which she would get busy preparing with an abundance of love.

I remember the run up to the meal vividly. While the rest of us sat around on charpoys, she would bustle around, efficiently sticking rotis inside the *chulha* and simultaneously cooking the saag. We would then be served the rotis with steaming hot sarson ka saag and fresh, thinly sliced mooli. It was food at its rustic best, simple and full of flavour, and even today, when winter arrives, I crave that saag and the innocence of that time. If I am visiting my parents in Delhi, I ask them to prepare sarson ka saag.

My father too craves his mother's saag, and a couple of times a year, during winter, when the market is flush with the tenderest saag, he takes over the kitchen and prepares the dish for the family. He doesn't let anyone else cook the saag because he wants to do it his way, with his own seasoning, which features loads of garlic. Ma is happy to play second fiddle, cutting and chopping and prepping for Papa to make his grand entry.

His 'sarson ka saag day' is now almost a ritual in the family and everyone, including my little niece, participates in it. It is hard to believe but at just six years of age, my niece has developed a taste for it because it is part of our household food. And that is just as it should be.

I will also always cherish memories of visiting my bua and her family at Bachhlauta, another village in Uttar Pradesh. Bua had four daughters and two sons, and the family had a quaint village home where the cattle was kept in the *aangan* (courtyard) as part of the family.

I will never forget the carefree times my sister and I spent with the family, the highlight of which was roaming around in the fields surrounding the village.

For me, the visit to Bua's home was also about eating the most delicious shakkar kandi (sweet potatoes). Bua stocked the fresh shakkar kandi, brought right after the harvest, in a storehouse within the compound of her house. Sometimes, when my parents would be lolling on the charpoys chatting with the seniors, we would head to the fields with Bua and look for the tenderest shakkar kandi, which she would roast on a coal fire. I still remember the fragrance of the smoky shakkar kandi, freshly toasted, sweet and juicy, which we ate with a whole chilly crushed into rock salt with a squeeze of lemon juice on top. Even today, when I see shakkar kandi, I am transported right back to my perch atop a tree stump or a large stone in the middle of the fields, devouring it with gusto. And the memory is so strong that I cannot bring myself to eat shakkar kandi boiled or as chips or in any other form!

Bua's village was also where we roamed around plucking fresh bhutta (corn) from the fields and then head to the nearest house that had a lit fire, on which we would roast it. We would eat the corn right there. In villages, chulhas are lit only once in the morning for breakfast before everybody heads to the fields to work and again in the evening, for dinner.

Ma was a fabulous cook who really practised the farm-to-table concept in her cooking much before it became a fashionable thing to do. In our kitchen garden in Karnal where we lived, she grew everything—from beans, corn, sugar cane, potatoes to onions, brinjal, gourds and garlic—and fed her kids and husband the freshest food possible. My sister learnt a lot of cooking from Ma but I remained a wanderer, gathering dried flowers, twigs, berries and leaves to make beautiful arrangements for the house. I would also happily fetch vegetables for Ma from the garden, but I never bothered to learn cooking from her.

Ma loved simple cooking but her food always stood out because it was full of flavour. My sister and I got treated to simple, tasty fare on our birthdays—palak, methi, mirchi, baingan, aloo or kele ke patte ke pakode and her signature paneer pakode with a layer of masala in between two chunks of paneer. Birthday treats could not get better than that.

We also got home-made potato chips. She sliced, parboiled and dried the potatoes on our terrace and stored them to be fried and eaten as a snack on special occasions and celebrations. And even though I have eaten potato fries and wedges in so many countries, nothing compares to the taste of Ma's aloo ke chips. Her gulab jamuns were the tastiest, and I remember she used to even make us doughnuts at home all those decades ago.

It is funny how we keep going back to the food from our childhood. When I visit my parents in Delhi now, I ask Ma to prepare her dal khichdi for me. When I eat it with ghee and dahi, it feels like she has enveloped me in a warm hug.

Now that my son, Rudra, is growing up, I feel I too should cook for him so he knows what our food is all about. I am learning Punjabi chole, dal khichdi and other staples from Ma. I had guests over recently, and I found myself making the same kheer that Papa used to make when I was a little kid. Ma would visit my maternal grandparents in Delhi whenever one of them was not keeping well or needed some assistance. Papa would then take charge of the kitchen, and even if there was nothing else, I remember eating a lot of his divine rice kheer. It is one of the most comforting foods that takes me back to my childhood, and I feel warm, secure and comforted, almost as if my parents are near me. For his seventy-sixth birthday this year, I made the kheer for him, and he was delighted that I was carrying his legacy forward.

When I shifted to Delhi for my higher education, I would often visit my maternal grandparents. Nani was a woman with multiple interests—painting, crochet, knitting, among other things. Her sooji ka halwa (semolina halwa) was incomparable. My stint in Delhi brought me very close to her. She was ageing by then and was unable to cook much, but she taught me how to, supervising and giving me instructions. She taught me how to make the perfect dough for rotis. When Rudra appreciates my rotis, I am reminded of my days in her kitchen, she overseeing as I kneaded the dough. She had magic in her hands. Her parathas with ghee were so flaky and delicious that I could never stop at just one.

Nani made the best pickles ever and Ma has picked up that skill from her. Nani's kitchen featured shelves upon shelves of different pickles, arranged according to their vintage. She insisted that her nimbu achaar had medicinal properties and she would give it to her children and grandchildren to cure ailments ranging from acidity to stomach ache and indigestion. Ma's house also has a cupboard full of achaars, of which her aam ka achaar and meetha achaar are my favourites.

It warms my heart today when I see how Rudra loves spending time with his grandparents. As a young mother, when I travelled for work, I would entrust him to my mother's care and he developed a bond with her over simple food like rajma chawal and dal chawal.

At my mother-in-law's place in Allahabad, he watches her make kachori and parathas, and he has developed a taste for her kind of food. She is passionate about cooking, and her life revolves around planning the menu. She learnt everything from Ammaji, her mother-in-law, and is keen to keep that tradition alive. Her happiest moments are when she is cooking for my husband and son.

My favourite meal today is a simple fare of rice, dal, dahi, pickle and papad. For years, I did not really cook, but these days I find myself spending some time cooking and it sparks so much joy when Rudra joins me and enjoys cooking with me. I am revisiting the simpler way of life, slowing down, going for a walk with my son like we used to with our parents. Connecting with my sister and Ma over food and their collection of time-tested recipes is a part of this new way of living.

DAHI BHALLE

Ingredients

- 1 bowl urad dal
- 1-inch piece of ginger
- A pinch of asafoetida
- Salt and chilli powder to taste
- Oil for frying
- 1 large bowl of thickish yoghurt, whisked
- Mint chutney
- Sweet and sour dates and jaggery chutney
- Black salt and roasted cumin powder for garnishing
- Coriander leaves for garnishing (optional)

Method

- Soak the urad dal for 3 hours, grind to a coarse paste, add a pinch of asafoetida and keep overnight in fridge.
- Add crushed ginger to this mixture along with salt and red chilli powder.
- Heat the oil and fry small vadas till golden.
- Toss the vadas into a bowl of cold water soon after removing them from the frying pan.
- To serve, add the vadas to a bowl of chilled thickish yogurt beaten well with a little water.

- To this add roasted cumin powder, black salt, green mint chutney and a sweet and sour chutney of dates and jaggery.

GREEN MINT CHUTNEY

Ingredients

- 1 small bunch of coriander leaves (2 cups)
- 1 quarter of a bunch of mint leaves
- 2 cloves of garlic
- 3 green chillies
- 1 tsp lemon juice or as preferred
- 1/4 tsp sugar
- Salt as preferred

Method

- Wash all the ingredients and grind them in the mixer. The lemon juice will give the chutney a fresh green colour.
- Keep it in an airtight container in the fridge, to be used in chaats, dahi vadas or sandwiches.
- You can also prepare this in a larger quantity and freeze. To use, simply take out required quantity a few hours before you need it and mix well.

DATE, TAMARIND AND JAGGERY CHUTNEY

Ingredients

- 1/2 cup seedless dates chopped, soaked in water for an hour and pulped with the back or a spoon or by hand

- 1/2 cup jaggery crushed or grated
- 1/4 cup pulp of soaked tamarind
- 1/2 tsp each red chilli powder, coriander powder, roasted cumin powder
- Salt as preferred

Method

- Boil the dates, tamarind pulp and jaggery with 2–3 cups of water for around 10 minutes, then add salt and all the spices.
- Boil for another 10 minutes and then simmer for 5.
- Let it cool, keep it in a glass jar and store in the fridge. If you want a smooth consistency for the chutney you can blend it in a mixer.

SARSON KA SAAG

Ingredients

- 1 kg sarson leaves
- 250 gm bathua (goosefoot or pigweed) leaves
- 10–12 garlic cloves
- 1-inch piece of ginger
- 3 green chillies
- 1/2 cup corn flour
- Asafoetida and salt as per preference

Method

- Wash the leaves well in running water and chop finely.

- Put all the ingredients together in a pressure cooker and boil for half an hour.
- Once boiled, add 1/2 cup of corn flour, 1 cup of water and keep on simmer, mixing well, on a low flame for 10–15 minutes.
- Once done, put off the flame and mix the saag well with a mathani (traditional wooden whisk).
- We never use a mixer to blend the saag because it becomes pasty.
- Finish with a seasoning of chopped garlic fried in ghee.

SURPRISE PUDDING

Ingredients

- 500 gm milk
- 10 pieces Glucose biscuits
- 125 gm paneer
- 6 pieces wafers (pineapple /orange / chocolate)
- Sugar as per preference
- Powder of 2 cardamoms
- Cherries for garnishing
- Dry fruits, such as cashew nuts, pistachios, almonds and raisins.

Method

- Bring milk to boil, mix in the powdered glucose biscuits made into a paste with a little milk, crushed wafers and keep stirring for 5 minutes to avoid lumps.
- Then add grated paneer and keep stirring for another 5 minutes.

* Once the dish starts to thicken, add sugar, then the dry fruits and finish with the cardamom powder.
* Once cool, place the dish in the refrigerator and garnish with cherries before serving.

ANUPAM BANERJEE, MICHELIN-STARRED CHEF AND DIRECTOR OF FOOD AND BEVERAGE, THE ST. REGIS BEIJING

MOTHER: MEERA BANERJEE

The image of Ma tending our kitchen garden, talking to the plants and humming her songs will always be part of the memories of the food I ate growing up. When my parents moved out of their joint family home and built their own house closer to the college where my mother worked, she insisted that she wanted a garden to grow vegetables, fruits and herbs that she could use in her cooking.

The meals she served us would always have freshly plucked produce from the garden she passionately looked after—brinjal, capsicum, chillies, green leafy vegetables, lemon, mint, coriander, tulsi and a lot of fruits. Eating that simple fare—steamed or fried fish, panchphoran dal, aloo poshto—shaped my philosophy about food when I become a chef: keep it simple, keep it fresh and keep it local.

Ma was a lecturer in economics at Ranchi University and in between raising three children, tending the house and focusing on teaching, she always ensured we were all happy when we ate at the dining table. This is what I tell my teams wherever I work: Cook like you are cooking for your family and serve food that will make everyone happy, without any complaints. This insight has always stood me in good stead.

Since she was busy on weekdays, all of us would look forward to breakfast on weekends when she would make our favourite luchis with aloo subzi. Sometimes the luchis would be accompanied by kheer and that was a bonus we loved. Lunch was exciting as well—rice, fried brinjal or padval (whatever was available in the garden), dal and soya nuggets made with aloo or keema, our favourite dish at that time. There was a phase when us kids didn't eat a meal without soya nuggets, and Ma had mastered a dozen different ways to cook it. On weekends, she would always cook fish and meat. If she made her finger-licking good fish curry on Saturday, then lunch on Sunday would be meat and fried fish.

On weekends, Baba would set out in the morning to the fishmonger who kept the best fish aside for him because they had struck a great equation. I often accompanied him on these trips and was fascinated listening to their discussions on the best cuts of meat, etc. A decade later, when I became a chef, I always made it a point to develop a network of vendors who supplied me with the best produce for my restaurants.

During season, Baba would buy lots of green peas and all of us would peel them while watching TV. Later, Ma would magically transform them into mouth-wateringly sumptuous matar parathas. Sometimes, if there was mooli in the garden, there would be mooli parathas for breakfast or dinner, along with freshly set curd.

Ma's side of the family was big—they were eight siblings— and when they all got together, it was a giant gastronomic affair, with each family preparing its own specialty such as pulao, fish or mutton curry and delicious desserts. My nani was a constant learner in the kitchen and all her experiments found their way into our stomachs with much happy results. I particularly remember this incident where I had to stay at her house when the rest of the family was travelling. I was around twelve years old, but I was in charge of her and that made me feel very important. Nani took her role as chief nurturer of her eldest grandson very seriously, plying me with the most amazing food from breakfast to dinner. I still remember the taste of her fish curries and believe me when I say that no one can prepare fish the way she could. One day, she was experimenting in the kitchen and made something peculiar—a dish with tomatoes, potatoes and green peas into which she added some papad. I was startled when I opened my tiffin box at school. I was not sure I liked it much but the taste stayed with me for some days. Imagine my own surprise when, a few days later, I found myself requesting her to make the same dish again! That is how it works with food. Experimenting is a must if you want to develop your palate.

Most of us have fond childhood memories around food. From lessons learnt at the kitchen counter to family dramas around dining tables, families, food and fond memories seem to be inextricably linked. Many of my childhood memories were made in my grandmother's kitchen in Bengal.

I think my decision to become a chef was shaped by the exposure to so many different kinds of food made by my extended family, but even so, it was a difficult decision to make. The initial reaction when I announced my decision to follow a career in food was of shock because everyone in Ma's family were professors and academics and most people in Baba's family were engineers. A *bawarchi* (cook) in the family was unheard of but eventually everyone came around, and I have never regretted my decision to follow my heart.

Festivals were a big thing in our family and the get-togethers were special, especially the extended puja festival when we would hop from family lunches and dinners to pandals where I enjoyed the khichdi meals a lot. I still cannot understand how the women of the house managed to put together such elaborate meals during the festival.

We travelled once a year to visit relatives in other cities, and I remember the food that travelled with us would be snacks like puffed rice and aloo bhaja, paratha or pooris and pickles for main meals. We siblings never liked that we had to eat home-made stuff on the train because we wanted to eat all the tempting stuff available at various railway stations. We would fight over who got to sit by the window, and all of us would sulk until Baba would realize that we wanted to eat snacks bought from vendors on the station and relent. Ma would be happy we got a treat, but she always felt that home-made food was the best.

In the three decades since I left home, I have lived in the remotest corners of the world and eaten in some of the best restaurants, but I still wait for the day when I go home and eat a simple meal cooked by Ma and served with love. No meal on earth can compare with it.

JHAL MURI

Ingredients

- 2 cups puffed rice
- 1/4 cup chanachur (fried gram, salted and spiced)
- 1/4 cup sev (Bengal gram vermicelli)

- 3 tbs peanuts (roasted or pan-fried and drained on paper towels)
- 2 tbs fresh and thinly sliced coconut
- 1 green chilli, finely chopped
- 1 small onion, finely chopped
- 1/2 tsp mustard oil
- 1/2 tsp oil
- Salt to taste

Method

- Mix all of the ingredients in a bowl.
- Season the mixture with salt to taste.
- Serve the jhal muri immediately in bowls so it does not get soggy.

SHORSE BATA MAACH

Ingredients

- 1 kg pabda fish
- 1/2 tbs turmeric powder
- 1 bunch fresh coriander leaves
- 50 ml mustard oil
- 1 tbs black cumin
- 3 green chillies, slit

For grinding

- 25 gm yellow mustard seeds
- 25 gm black mustard seeds
- 7 green chillies
- Salt to taste

Method

- Clean the fish and pat it dry.
- Marinate with salt, 1 tsp oil and turmeric powder for 10 minutes.
- Heat 1 tsp oil in a *kadhai*, shallow fry the fish after covering with a lid and keep aside.
- Pour 2 tbs oil in the kadhai, add 1 tsp of black cumin and add the mustard and green chilli paste.
- Add 1 cup of hot water.
- When the gravy starts to boil, add the fried fish and let it simmer.
- When the fish is cooked, garnish it with coriander leaves and simmer for 5 more minutes.

MA'S GHUGNI PAV

Ingredients

- 2 cups dried yellow peas soaked, drained and boiled
- 2 tbs oil
- 1 medium-sized onion, chopped
- 1/2 tsp cumin seeds
- 1 bay leaf
- 1 tsp ginger, finely chopped
- 1/4 tsp turmeric powder
- 1 medium tomato, chopped
- 2 tsp roasted cumin powder
- 1/4 cup slices of fresh coconut
- 2 green chillies slit
- 1/2 tsp garam masala powder
- Salt to taste

Method

- ◆ Heat oil in a non-stick pan.
- ◆ Add cumin seeds, bay leaf and chopped onion and sauté till lightly browned. Add ginger, turmeric powder, tomato and a little water and mix. Sauté till the tomato becomes pulpy.
- ◆ Add peas and mix well.
- ◆ Add 1/4 cup of water and salt.
- ◆ Add cumin powder and coconut slices and mix well.
- ◆ Add green chillies, garam masala powder and mix. Cover and cook on medium heat for 5 minutes. Serve hot with toasted pav.

ANURAAG BHATNAGAR, CHIEF OPERATING OFFICER, THE LEELA PALACES, HOTELS AND RESORTS

MOTHER: URMILA BHATNAGAR

I will always remember my childhood days, of Sunday mornings spent at home in Faridabad, where my engineer dad was posted in the late 1970s and 1980s. Those were the days of *Illustrated Weekly* and Khushwant Singh's no-holds-barred columns, and with Dad at home, the newspapers spread around him, there would be heated discussions on politics.

All three of us—Dad, my sister and I—would look forward to breakfast on Sundays, because Mom would always have a treat planned: eggs made in different ways; her signature aloo, gobhi or mooli parathas; or, bread roll stuffed with potatoes, cucumber and spices, deep fried and served with mint chutney. It was heavenly to bite into the rolls, crispy on the outside and bursting with flavour inside.

The family ritual was that after breakfast Dad would go to the market to pick up the choicest cuts of meat from his regular mutton shop. I would accompany him faithfully, watching in fascination as he skilfully negotiated for an extra kaleji (mutton liver). The mutton vendor would part with it only because Dad was a regular customer.

When he returned, we knew there would be the usual argument between Mom and him on how to cook the mutton. He had very strong views on how to cook the curry and so did she. But eventually they would arrive at a consensus and everyone would be happy because Mom was such a wonderful cook and lent magic to whatever she touched.

Being a family of food lovers from Bareilly in Uttar Pradesh, our meal times were all about appreciating and enjoying every morsel that went down our throats.

It was easy to be entranced by Mom's cooking because she always had a way with food and her Punjabi background brought an unusual regional flavour to the largely UP fare cooked at home. All of us loved her mutton curry on weekends, the mid-week biryani treat and her crispy, stuffed bhindi any time of the week. It's been years since I left home to travel around the world for work, but I am yet to find a bhindi fry that comes even close to the one she makes. I have always wondered what spices go into the filling of the bhindi but have never got around to asking her.

Dad loved his mutton curry, while Mom was very fond of keema matar (keema with peas), but because the family favoured the former, keema matar became an accompaniment, never the star dish of the meal. Mom started making it as a special dish when there were guests at home. Visitors at home also meant finger-licking good biryani, UP style. Mom's best-loved dishes were and continue to be mutton curry and mutton rogan josh. And even today, my mouth waters when I think of the 'tiffin' she would have waiting for us when we returned from school—Mumbai toasties, which were basically buttered and grilled sandwiches with potatoes and spicy chutneys inside. Some days we were treated to her signature kaleji masala and the fun part of this was that we got to taste the dish as she was preparing it, because she wanted to make sure everything was perfect when it was finally done!

Mom never had to trick us into eating our daily portions of vegetables—her vegetarian dishes were so delicious that we relished every bit and even asked for more!

Growing up, our friends could never believe that my siblings and I actually loved arbi and karela and requested Mom to make them often. There was not a single person in our class who ate karela, but Mom's stuffed karela, rich with its secret stuffing of sweet and tart spices, all sewn together to make plump parcels to be deep fried, had us begging for more. That recipe is a family favourite even today.

We are not a family with a sweet tooth, but in winters we looked forward to her kaddu halwa and delicious Punjabi-style gajar halwa, the latter cooked to retain the crunch in the grated carrot, unlike the pasty halwa we find in restaurants.

Eating together on Sunday was a ritual back then, and we would spend an hour, sometimes two, just chatting and listening to our parents' conversations as Mom kept up a steady stream of phulkas, hot off the tawa. There would always be three to four dishes on the table—a dal, a couple of vegetables and a non-vegetarian dish. Today, all this seems like such a luxury.

Even today, when everyone is busy with their lives in Mumbai, we make sure to have at least one meal at home on Sunday, and the cherry on the cake is when my parents join us to make the occasion extra special. Mom is ageing now and does not cook that much, but on special occasions, she still gets into the kitchen, and we can't wait for her to finish cooking some of our childhood treats.

KURKURE BHINDI

Ingredients

* 1/2 kg bhindi
* 2 or 3 large onions
* Salt as per preference
* Coriander powder as per preference
* Red chilli powder as per preference
* Haldi as per preference
* Amchur as per preference
* Fennel powder to taste
* 1/2 tsp mustard seeds
* 1/2 tsp fenugreek seeds
* 2 tbs mustard oil

Method

* Wash and dry the bhindi on a towel.
* Cut into small roundels or slivers.
* Finely chop the onion and fry till crispy brown in mustard oil. Remove from the oil.
* Add fenugreek seeds to the oil. Let them splutter. Now add the chopped bhindi and mix well.
* Keep the flame low. Add salt and cover the pan with a lid. Cook for 3 to 4 minutes. Remove the cover and add coriander powder, turmeric and chilli powder. Let it fry for two to three minutes uncovered. Add fried onion, amchur powder and fennel powder. Keep tossing the bhindi for

a few minutes. You will notice that all the dry spices and the fried onion will start to stick to the bhindi and it will start turning crispy. The more you pan roast it, the better the taste.

◆ Serve with rotis or as a side for rice.

MUTTON MASALA

Ingredients

◆ 1 kg mutton
◆ 1/2 kg onions
◆ 1-inch piece ginger
◆ 4–5 pods of garlic
◆ 4 medium-sized tomatoes
◆ 1 bowl (approximately 50 gm) curd
◆ 1 1/2 tbs ghee
◆ 1 tsp cumin seeds
◆ 5–6 black peppercorns
◆ 2 medium-sized bay leaves
◆ 3–4 pods black cardamom
◆ Salt to taste
◆ 1 tsp garam masala
◆ 1 tbs coriander powder
◆ 1/2 tsp turmeric powder
◆ Chilli powder and Kashmiri mirch powder for rich red colour (as per taste)
◆ Dry kasoori methi (dry fenugreek leaves) or dry pudina (mint)

Method

◆ Wash the mutton and keep aside.

- Slice a large onion into thin, long strips.
- Fry the sliced onion in ghee till it browns. Remove and keep it aside.
- Blend the remaining onion, ginger and garlic into a smooth paste.
- Blend the tomatoes into a smooth paste.
- Heat the ghee used for frying the onions. Now add the whole spices (cumin, bay leaves, cardamom, black pepper, etc.) to it. Add the onion paste. Fry it for 10 minutes till it starts to change colour.
- Now add mutton to it and fry it for another 10–15 minutes.
- Keep it covered all the time so that the aroma of the spices gets infused into the mutton and does not escape.
- Add the tomato paste along with all the remaining spices.
- Keep frying the mutton with all the ingredients.
- All the roasting/sautéing should be on low heat. Once the extra ghee starts oozing from the masala, add the curd and fried onion.
- Keep frying. The more you roast it in the masala, the better it tastes, as this allows all the spices to seep into the meat.
- When the masala is nicely fried, with the extra oil forming a layer on the surface, check that the mutton is cooked to your preference, and then sprinkle either dry pudina or dry kasoori methi.
- Check the tenderness of the meat. Add water to your liking. If the meat needs more cooking, then steam it in a pressure cooker or just keep it covered after adding water and let it simmer for 15–20 minutes.
- Garnish it with finely chopped coriander leaves. Serve hot with chapattis, naan or tandoori roti.

BHUNI KALEJI MASALA

Ingredients

- 1/2 kg fresh kaleji
- 1-inch piece ginger
- 4–5 cloves of garlic
- 1/2 kg onion
- 3 deseeded green chillies
- 1 tsp cumin seeds
- 6–7 black peppercorns
- 3–4 black cardamom
- 3–4 green cardamom
- 2 medium-sized bay leaves
- 3 tsp dhania powder
- Chilli powder as per preference
- Garam masala as per preference
- 2 tbs refined oil
- Salt to taste

Method

- Wash and cut kaleji into medium-sized pieces.
- Finely chop ginger, garlic, onions and green chillies.
- Take some oil in a pan.
- Fry ginger and remove it from the pan.
- Now add whole spices with the chopped garlic. Fry till it changes colour slightly.
- Add chopped onions. Fry for 5–6 minutes till they change colour.
- Add kaleji and green chilli. Cover the pan.

- After a few minutes, add all the remaining spices. Cover and simmer on low fire till the kaleji is coated with the masala.
- Add a little water to cook the kaleji.
- Once it is soft, squeeze lemon juice and garnish with fried ginger and fresh coriander before serving.

ASHWINI IYER TIWARI, FILM DIRECTOR

MOTHER: LATA IYER

The one thing that stands out in my mind about my mother's food from my childhood is her adventurous streak and her penchant for all things new. Amma loved street food and we would often walk over to the neighbourhood vendors to gorge on her favourites—vada pav, dabeli, Sindhi pav. In fact, my fondest memory of the time when Dad was abroad for work was our Friday evening routine—she would make vada pavs and we would demolish quite a few between us. Sizzling hot vadas, smeared with lasoon chutney, and pressed into the softest pavs.

When I look back, I wonder how she managed all of that because she was a working woman, a teacher with long hours at school, but she managed to keep me well fed at all times. Amma was different from the other south Indian moms who cooked traditional south Indian fare for their families. I had a bone to pick with her because I would often want to eat the traditional south Indian food that my grandma and periamma (maternal aunt) made, but she was not as good as they were in that department. Maybe that was because of the years she spent with Dad in other parts of the world before eventually deciding to raise me in India so that she could work and also school me here. We lived in a middle-class, cosmopolitan community in Mulund, then a growing suburb of Mumbai, which was perfect for her interest in different kinds of food.

She perfected dhokla and handvo from our Gujarati neighbours, and learnt how to make the perfect baingan ka bharta from the parents of my Punjabi friends. 'I became a good cook because of you,' she would sometimes say.

But what I love from her repertoire is the traditional Palakkad Iyer south Indian cuisine. Her cheera molakootal with rice and chammandi (chutney, often with coconut) make me salivate and so does her pulinji. When she visits me these days, the kids and I pull her in different directions, and I end up squabbling with her because she prepares their favourites instead of making some molakootal for me! To most non-south Indians, molakootal might seem like dal-palak, but it is not. The perfect molakootal comes from years of practice. Nitesh (husband, director Nitesh Tiwari) often sees me polishing off the molakootal and asks: 'What is that green thing you are eating?' and I tell him, 'You north Indians won't ever appreciate the taste of this!' But he too waits for Amma to visit so that he and the kids can eat idli, vada, chutney and sambar.

One of my other favourites from Amma's kitchen was and continues to be her red pumpkin vathakozhambu, a dish that is uniquely south Indian and an acquired taste. Amma makes it for me occasionally and now, seventeen years after I got married and left home, she finally remembers that I hate whole fenugreek in my vathakozhambu! Vathakozhambu with ghee and fried pappadams was my idea of heaven in my teenaged years. Amma also made a great lemon rice and her thogayal continues to be a favourite of mine. I have tried my hand at making the typical Palakkad thogayal, but it is never quite the same as hers, and I suspect she is tickled when she hears me say that.

My food memories from my growing-up years also prominently feature my grandma and my periamma, both formidable cooks, whom I admire immensely, causing my mother some annoyance, I suspect. I told Amma there were some things she could never prepare as well as Grandma or Periamma. For instance, nobody makes chetthu manga kari or finely chopped mango pickle as well as my periamma. This is a simple instant pickle of finely chopped raw mangoes in red chilli powder with very little oil, but she added such grace to it, cutting it beautifully and spicing it just right. Even the colour of the red chilli powder she used was perfect. We also call this the kalyanam mango pickle, because it is an essential part of every south Indian wedding feast.

My supply of kadumangai, or baby mangoes in thin, spicy, salt water, has to come from my grandmother because she gets the balance of spicy, sour and salty just right. Amma makes a great avakkai mango pickle.

Amma has perfected a few south Indian recipes, and no one makes it quite like she does. Her lemon rice, sambar and pulinji—a thick, sour, tart preparation of tamarind pulp and lots of ginger and jaggery—are divine and so is her molagapodi. I like how her molagapodi is a bit grainy unlike the shop-bought gun powder that is finely ground and has no character to it. When she visits me, she either carries my supply of molagapodi or makes it for me at home.

The rice papads she makes with red chilli powder sometimes is an all-time favourite snack and even though it is deep fried, I cannot resist munching on one of these with a cup of chai. As a child, I would often hang around her when she would prepare this in bulk for the year and the bonus for this would be that I got to break off chunks from the huge ball of dough and eat it right there, dipped in til oil. When she visits us these days, she carries all sorts of delicious junk like packaged chips and fruit drinks for my children and kilos of these papads and karuvadams for me. This is my guilty pleasure unlimited.

Festival time in our house was exciting, and I used to look forward to Amma making neiappams—sweet jaggery appams fried in ghee—and the 'mixture', a typical south Indian savoury, which was so good that none of the store-bought ones make the cut for me today. She has always had a huge sweet tooth and so maa ladoo and rawa ladoo were made in abundance. Such is her fondness for sweet things that at tea time she suddenly disappears into the kitchen and comes out with a plateful of glorious, moist, glistening jaggery-and-coconut-infused poha.

When you travel with Amma, you have to make peace with the fact that she carries a lot of food cleverly tucked away inside her luggage so that no one notices. Among the things she must carry with her at all times are her signature sweet potato chips and molagapodi. On a recent trip to Mizoram, I realized the value of her molagapodi. There was not much vegetarian food that the kids wanted to eat, and they were grumpy and hungry. Out came Amma's suitcase and from it emerged her container of molagapodi that she cleverly served them with bread slices and butter. The kids could not have enough of it. I have now decided that I will not argue with her when she insists on carrying her staple food items along on our trips.

Amma believes that the cure to all problems and ailments is eating a generous portion of thayir sadam—curd rice. She really does believe that eating this magical dish cures coughs and colds, and if someone has eaten up all your hair, thayir sadam will still work wonders.

RECIPES FROM AMMA (LATA) AND PERIAMMA (GEETA)

VATHAKOZHAMBU

Ingredients

* Lemon-sized ball of tamarind
* 1 tbs dried chundakkai (Turkey berry)
* 1/2 tsp turmeric powder
* 6 curry leaves
* 1 tsp mustard seeds
* 2 red chillies
* 1/2 tsp urad dal
* 1/4 tsp hing
* 1/2 tsp chana dal
* 4 tsp til oil
* Salt to taste

To be roasted and powdered fine

* 1 tbs dhania
* 2 tsp urad dal
* 1 tsp pepper corns
* 2 tsp chana dal
* 1/2 tsp methi
* 4 red chillies
* 1/4 tsp jeera

Method

- Soak the tamarind in hot water and extract the pulp.
- Heat oil in a kadhai, add mustard seeds and when they start to splutter, add dals, chillies, chundakkai, hing and curry leaves.
- Add tamarind pulp, salt to taste, haldi and 2 heaped tsp of the powdered spices. Stir and boil well. Let it simmer.
- To thicken the gravy you could add 1 tsp of rice flour mixed with water. When the oil floats on the gravy, remove from the stove.
- Serve with steaming hot rice, roasted pappadams or karuvadams.

KEERAI MOLAKOOTAL

Ingredients

- 1 bunch methi leaves or spinach
- 1 cup tuvar or moong dal
- 1/2 tsp haldi
- 1/2 cup grated coconut
- 1/4 tsp red chilli powder
- 1/4 tsp jeera
- Salt to taste
- 1 tsp rice flour

For seasoning

- 2 tsp coconut oil
- 1 tsp mustard seeds

- 1/2 tsp urad dal
- 1/4 tsp jeera

Method

- Wash and soak the dal for 1/2 hour and pressure cook. Then mash well and keep aside.
- Wash the greens under running water and chop them finely.
- Cook the greens with haldi and red chilli powder without adding any water. Keep aside to cool.
- In a mixer jar, add coconut, jeera, rice flour and water and grind it to a fine paste.
- In a vessel, blend the cooked greens coarsely. Add coconut paste, mix well and let it simmer for 5–10 minutes. Add the cooked tuvar dal and boil for a further 10 minutes.
- Add water if necessary. Remove it from the stove.
- Heat coconut oil in a kadhai, add mustard seeds, and as they splutter, add urad dal and fry till it is golden brown.
- Add keerai molakootal.
- Serve with rice, pickles and papads.

THOGAYAL

Ingredients

- 1 tbs urad dal
- 2 or 3 red chillies
- 1/2 tsp hing
- 1 tbs oil
- 1/2 cup fresh grated coconut
- A lemon-sized ball of tamarind
- Salt to taste

Method

- Heat oil in a kadhai and fry the urad dal, chillies and hing. Let it cool.
- Coarsely grind grated coconut, tamarind, salt and the roasted ingredients, adding very little water.
- Remove it in a bowl and serve.
- Goes well with molakootal, curd rice, dosa and as a tasty sandwich spread.

MAA LADOO

Ingredients

- 1 cup skinned, roasted Bengal gram (pottu kadalai)
- 1 cup sugar
- 1 tbs chopped cashew nuts
- 1 tbs raisins
- 1/2 tsp cardamom powder
- 1/2 cup ghee

Method

- Dry roast the dal for 2 minutes. Allow it to cool.
- Mix the sugar and dal and grind them to a fine powder and put it in a vessel.
- Heat 2 tsp ghee in a kadhai and add the cashew nuts. As they change colour, add the raisins. When they puff up, pour over the ground mixture.
- In the same kadhai, add the remaining ghee and let it melt. Keep aside.
- Pour the ghee, a little at a time over the powder and mix well.

- Add cardamom powder.
- As you mix the powder, form lemon-sized ladoos in your greased palms. If it opens and falls apart, add a little more ghee. Mix well and make the remaining ladoos.
- Your tasty maa ladoos are ready to eat and can be stored for a couple of weeks in an airtight container.

ATUL DODIYA, ARTIST

MOTHER: NANDKUVAR DODIYA

Growing up in Ghatkopar, a suburb in Mumbai, where we lived in a chawl in great harmony with several Maharashtrian families, Ba (my mother) had adopted the practice of fasting in the month of Shravan. She asked the rest of the family to fast too, on Mondays of the month. The fast involved eating only one meal, usually at night, and faral (fasting snacks) during the day. I remember waiting eagerly for Shravan Mondays because Ba would prepare delicious *upvas* (fasting) snacks for lunch. I adored her sukhi potato bhajis, fried sakkariyas (sweet potato), rajgira (amaranth) puris, fried peanuts garnished with roasted jeera powder, all washed down with fresh dahi. I could eat great quantities of these snacks to Ba's endless amusement.

Ours was a middle-class household and Ba was a simple woman from Kathiawad, Gujarat, who cooked a simple fare of rustic Kathiawadi food—dal, chawal, rotli, shaak—for her husband and seven children. Since I was the first son born to her after four daughters, my siblings always teased her that the household had to eat whatever her pampered son wanted to eat.

Unlike the rest of Gujarat where food is sweet, Kathiawadi food is spicy with lots of chillies, onion and garlic in it. Ba, a keen learner, always ready to experiment, eventually learnt how to balance the spice in her preparations, taking away the raw, rustic side to it. Ba was from a Rajput family and had in her repertoire of recipes a number of non-vegetarian dishes, but strangely enough, I have no memory of her eating non-vegetarian food at home. My parents gave up non-vegetarian food at some point in my childhood and we grew up on a largely vegetarian fare.

While lunch at home was always the typical rotli, dal and shaak made Kathiawadi style from vegetables such as bitter gourd, cabbage and cauliflower, dinner was when the entire family sat down to have a meal of thick bajra bhakris with dollops of ghee and a gravy-based vegetable because the bhakris were too dry to be eaten on their own. Dinner also had Ba's delectable moong dal khichdi with lots of ghee, a taste that still lingers in my memory, reminding me of her.

Ba's cabbage and potato shaak was one of my favourites, as was a karela dish with roasted masalas and onions, which was so delicious that we kids would actually look forward to her cooking it. She also made an outstanding drumstick dish with a thick gravy of besan, and I remember dipping my rotlis into the gravy, soaking them up and popping them into my mouth, steaming hot. She also prepared a variety of dals—chana, moong and urad—all of them spicy and yet comforting. On the side, with every meal, would be dry chilli pickle made from either red or green chillies.

I will never forget Saturday afternoons when I would come home from school by lunchtime, while my sisters would have classes till evening. Ba would wait for me so that she could serve me hot rotlis with a shaak she knew I liked. We would eat together and chat endlessly about school, film and music, both of which she loved.

Ba had a way with snacks, but I was particularly fond of her bhajiyas—made with potatoes, chillies and even sweet bananas. I could eat any number.

In summers, Ba would get busy making pickles. We Gujaratis have a variety of pickles, but she would make not just the usual mango and lemon pickles but also some very traditional ones that women in her hometown would make. Thus, our kitchen shelf would have jars of daalla, garmar (coleus root) and gunda (bird lime or fragrant manjack) pickles, things our modern households neither know, nor bother to make. Sometimes, when I visit my sister in Saurashtra, I get to taste these pickles. I especially remember Ba's gunda pickle. She and my sisters would dry the gundas in the sun for days before mixing them with mangoes, turmeric and spices. When I close my eyes, I can still picture her making the pickle and feel its unique taste in my mouth.

She loved festivals and celebrated them enthusiastically with the other families in our *wadi* (community). She would get really busy during Diwali when she would make pooris, ghogra, chakri and sankarpala, among other things. The festival of Sankranti in January particularly stands out in my memory because she would make delicious til and mamra (puffed rice) chikkis and til ladoos, which were distributed in the wadi. All the kids would come to our house for the ladoos because they knew she would have put 10 paise or 25 paise coins inside the ladoos as a surprise with which they could treat themselves to goodies. I still recall how excited my friends would be to find exactly how much money was hidden in their ladoos.

Ba was good at preparing a lot of traditional Gujarati dishes such as golpapdi. When there was a pooja at home, we would wait for her to make rawa sheera with ghee, badam and other dry fruits. The prasad ka sheera she made is the tastiest I have ever eaten.

On Sundays, she would make dhokla, which we would eat with a chutney made of oil, red chillies and garlic. My father would go across the street to a sweet shop and get fafda and jalebis to complete the breakfast. Lunch on Sundays would be special too—poori-bhaji and store-bought shrikhand. When we had guests, Ba would prepare doodh-pak and it was a feast all over again for us kids.

My birthdays were always special because Ba would make my favourite moong dal sheera, and after I had eaten, she would give me a Rs 100 note to buy art-related books that I loved. It is because of her encouragement that today I own one of the biggest art book collections in the country. She understood me and my love for reading. I would often bring the books home and read aloud to her, explaining the works of Picasso or Van Gogh.

Some days I miss the simplicity of the meals she made for us, but I know those times are long gone, and the new times have brought along pizza, pasta and meals ordered in and eaten while watching television.

KARELA

Ingredients

+ 5 to 6 karelas
+ 5 onions sliced long and thin
+ 2 small bowls of besan

- 1 tsp turmeric
- 3 tsp roasted coriander seed and cumin powder (dhaniya-jeera powder)
- Salt to taste
- 1/4 tsp mustard seeds
- 1/4 tsp fenugreek seeds
- A pinch of asafoetida for seasoning
- Curry leaves
- Coriander leaves
- 2 tsp sugar
- Juice of a lemon
- Garlic masala to taste: 4–5 pods of garlic, 1/2-inch piece of ginger and red chilli powder as per taste (made as follows: grind garlic, ginger, red chilli powder and salt to a fine paste. This chutney can be stored in the fridge in an air-tight container and used whenever required.)

Method

- Cut the karela into thin slices, add salt and keep it aside, preferably overnight.
- The next morning, wash them well and then boil them in a little water. Squeeze and discard the water.
- Heat oil in a pan, add mustard seeds, fenugreek seeds and curry leaves. When they start to splutter, add asafoetida and chopped onions.
- Simultaneously, mix the chickpea flour (besan) with all the masalas and then add it to the karela.
- Once the onions turn pink, add the karela mixed with the besan, masalas and sugar. Mix well.
- Cook this mixture in a pressure cooker for 2 whistles without adding any water. The bottom of the pressure

cooker needs to have the required quantity of water for its
safe functioning.

◆ After the pressure cooker has cooled down, gently stir
the karela, add coriander leaves and serve with a dash of
lemon juice.

CHOORMA KE LADOO

Ingredients

◆ 1 big cup wheat flour
◆ 2 small cups ghee
◆ 1/2 cup jaggery
◆ Poppy seeds (khuskhus) to taste
◆ Cardamom powder as preferred

Method

◆ Add 1/2 cup ghee to the wheat flour and knead till you
have a firm dough.
◆ Make this into 3 to 4 big and thick bhakris.
◆ Roast equally on both sides on a slow flame.
◆ Then grind these bhakris into a fine powder.
◆ To this chooran (bhakri powder), add cardamom powder
and mix well.
◆ Chop the jaggery into small, thin pieces and add it to the
mixture. Mix thoroughly.
◆ Now, warm the remaining ghee, and add it to the chooran,
kneading continuously.
◆ Mould this chooran into round balls, roll in a plate of khus
and the ladoos are ready to serve.

BHAJIYA

I know bhajiyas are fairly common in Indian kitchens, but I have added the recipe for it here because Ba knew I loved them. She would constantly experiment and improvise to give me a variety of bhajiyas.

Ingredients

+ 2 potatoes
+ 2 onions
+ 2 green plantains
+ 3–4 large chillies
+ 2 brinjals
+ A small bunch of spinach leaves, washed, drained and patted dry
+ Besan (chickpea flour), enough to make a thickish batter of pouring consistency to fry all of the above
+ 3 to 4 cloves of green garlic, crushed
+ Red chilli powder to taste
+ 1/2 tsp turmeric powder
+ Dhaniya and jeera powder to taste
+ Salt to taste
+ A pinch of cooking soda (optional)

Method

+ Add all the spices, garlic and salt to the besan. Make sure the batter has a thickish pouring consistency.
+ Slice potatoes, brinjals, onions and plantains.
+ Make lengthwise slits in the chillies.
+ Keep the spinach leaves intact.

- ◆ Heat oil in a kadhai.
- ◆ Dip each of the sliced vegetables, slit chillies and spinach leaves one by one in the batter and deep fry.
- ◆ Serve hot with green chutney.

ATUL KOCHHAR, LONDON-BASED MICHELIN-STARRED CHEF AND RESTAURATEUR

MOTHER: SUDESH KOCHHAR

Decades after I left home and shifted to London, I still crave the amazing aloo bujiya and namak-ajwain (caraway seeds) paratha that my mother made for breakfast before we headed out to school. I remember Mum used to wake up early, light the chulha and the first thing she would do after having her morning chai was make parathas. She would then fry finely chopped potatoes for the bujiya and the house would fill up with the aroma. Mum would get ready for work in the meantime, occasionally going to the kitchen to stir the bujiya. Later, she would use newspaper to wrap a couple of parathas each for her six children and pack the hot aloo bujiya in tiffin boxes.

Opening the tiffin box during lunch hour at school was the closest thing to heaven. The parathas would be a bit soggy from being packed hot in newspaper but the steam trapped in the lunch box also meant that the aloo bujiya would give off a glorious burst of aroma. I would greedily dig into it, scooping up the subzi with the parathas and gobbling it all up hungrily. I hated the fact that Mum was a teacher in our school and I would often have to eat my lunch in the staffroom, but the aloo bujiya lunches more than made up for it.

Since we lived in Jamshedpur, Mum's cooking was heavily influenced by Bihari cuisine, despite her being from a Punjabi family. Aloo bujiya and ajwain paratha were breakfast staples at home because they were simple to make, tasty and nutritious.

More than forty years later, I still salivate thinking about this meal, and when I cook it for my kids, they love it too. It takes me back to my childhood, when I was a seven-year-old boy in khaki shorts and white shirt, my green khadi bag slung across my shoulder, holding Mum's hand and walking to school. I talked about this to her a few years ago and she looked at me in surprise and laughed, saying she never realized I was so fond of her on-the-go breakfast staple.

For a large part of our childhood, Mum raised me and my five siblings—four sisters and a brother—by herself because Dad had set up his business in another city. We lived on the second floor of an old building and our apartment was split into two sections—the pooja room and the living room on one side and the kitchen and bedrooms on the other; a huge veranda joined the two sections. When it rained, we would have to dash across from one side to the other to avoid getting wet, but when Mum was in the kitchen, bustling around, getting our meals ready, we preferred to be around her or in the bedrooms.

Mum had this flair for making all kinds of lentils into memorable dishes. While rajma is a Punjabi dish that everybody loves, she would make an extraordinary dish out of its lesser-known cousin, black-eyed peas, or raungi, as it is called in Punjabi. It was the star of Sunday lunch at our home, because she had time on weekends to boil the beans for hours with onion and ginger-garlic paste and make a separate tomato masala for it to simmer in, so that all the flavours were soaked up by the beans. It was a summer dish that we ate with rice, and there would always be turai subzi on the side. I was always assigned the job of peeling the turai, and Mum would season it with cumin, garlic, green chillies, coriander powder, red chillies, turmeric powder and salt.

I absolutely loved her dal makhani and have combined her recipe with my grandma's to use in my restaurants, where the dish is much loved. I adored her chana dal preparation, but when she realized that, she started adding lauki to it because I hated lauki and would never eat it. She thought I would develop a liking for lauki along with the chana dal but instead I would pick out the lauki and simply eat the dal. She was a strict mom who insisted that we ate whatever was cooked at home. My refusal to eat the lauki in the dal led to a showdown between us. I was almost a teenager then, and I remember telling her I hated lauki. She said I would have to get used to it because that was all she could afford to feed us. For the next five days, Mom served the family lauki at every meal, including breakfast.

When I think about it today, I am awed at the genius of it. There was a different flavour, a new avatar of lauki on the table for every meal. One day she cooked lauki with wadis, another day there was lauki kofta, and on another there was lauki halwa. Her challenge then must have been twofold—she not only had to make me eat lauki but also make it interesting for the rest of the family who had to bravely eat it three times a day. If I had not given in by the fifth day, my sisters would have made mince out of me and eaten that, rather than one more meal of lauki!

When I remind her now, Mum says she has no recollection of this episode, but I know now that it was her love for me that made her do it. She was not trying to bore me with it; she was trying to make me appreciate that there was so much that could be made with lauki. That episode became a precious lesson for me, because I learnt to always accept whatever food was put on the table and eat it with gratitude.

Mum's cooking was simple and wholesome. There were no great flourishes in her kitchen. Her karela subzi was my absolute favourite; along with pooris and sookhe aloo ki subzi, it was also the family's travel staple. She had two sisters, one of whom lived in Ranchi, which was a couple of hours away from our home, and the other lived in Hazaribag, four to five hours away. We would often visit them. Since Mum hated us eating at roadside dhabas, our meal would travel with us—one portion each of karela, aloo and pooris packed neatly for each of us. I was a greedy kid back then and would barely wait for the bus to leave the terminal before wolfing down my portion of the food meant for the journey.

I have so many fond memories of travelling with Mum and my siblings to meet my grandma who lived in Dehradun. The journey took almost forty-eight hours in the early 1980s and meant changing a couple of trains, so the food would be packed a bit differently. Mum would get to work early on a pile of karelas, slitting and stuffing them with spices before deep frying the lot. She would then sprinkle her home-made powdered spices on top of the fried karela.

It wasn't easy to eat our meals sitting on the narrow berths on the train. Mum would hand out four to five pooris to each of us with some karela on top and aloo on the side. I remember we would eat it before the next station where we would get a hot cup of chai to wash it all down.

When Dad returned home to live with us after a few years, he jumped right into the kitchen. He was a terrific cook who had a catering business of his own. Two of my sisters had left for college by then, and the rest of us would take turns to cook with Mum and Dad.

We were a vegetarian family by choice. The norm of my mother's kitchen was to consume seasonal fruits and veggies. Mum was an amazing cook who applied her mind to convert the simplest food into memorable meals. I watched her almost our entire time together, how she had a way of adding spices—she would add whole spices first, then onions for body, then cook it to the right texture, adding the ginger garlic paste after the onions were done (or the flavour would change, she insisted). All of that came handy when I started learning professional cooking years later.

Holi was the biggest festival in our home, because we had the largest terrace in the apartment block we lived in. Some forty to fifty people would come to our house to celebrate. Celebrations would begin around 9 a.m. In those days, wet colours were only for kids and dry colours for adults. Any kid who tried to apply wet colour on an adult was tickled firmly.

In the afternoon, everybody would go home and return with a dish each for a giant community lunch. Mum would prepare huge amounts of gujiyas and malpuas and make a very special rose-flavoured nankhatai that her father, a baker, used to make. Mum would make them in a makeshift oven fashioned out of heavy steel *parats* (deep plates), with coal under and on top of them. Even though it was a tedious process, she loved doing it because everybody loved her nankhatais. Mum's dal makhani, another favourite among our neighbours, would also make it to the Holi lunch.

Work on the dal would begin very early in the morning, and it would simmer for hours on a low flame before it came to the table, aromatic and bubbling with desi ghee. These dishes find their way into my restaurant menus time to time, when I am overtaken by nostalgia.

Comfort food for me, on cold London days when I am feeling low and need cheering up, are the dizzying variety of Mum's parathas—missi roti, or aloo or ajawain paratha and a delicious chana dal. These simple recipes are special because they carry the scent of Mum and her kitchen.

Mum's kitchen had a cure for almost everything. Her turmeric milk stands out in my memory even today. If we had cough, cold, a bump or a scratch from a fall, out would come a hot cup of milk with turmeric in it. We would have to gulp it down whether we liked it or not. When I pay 5–6 pounds at a café in London for a turmeric latte, I laugh because this is a recipe that belongs to every mother in India.

Mum had lots of other remedies for when we were under the weather: toasted ajwain with black salt for tummy ache and gastric problems; for summer heat rash, she made a paste of neem leaves; almonds and aamchur were believed to be antiseptic, as was karela juice.

I think Mum learnt everything she knew about cooking from my nani who was a passionate cook. Mum had to possibly pick up the nuances of cooking very early because my grandma had a child every year (Mum had ten siblings) and so, by the time the last of her siblings were born, my mum was already in the kitchen, cooking for the family, under her mother's supervision. Mum is eighty-seven now and rarely cooks but we still have the benefit of her expertise in the kitchen. Now she gives us instructions when we want to make a particular dish that she used to excel in.

Her cooking has had a strong influence on mine. When I try something new in the kitchen I think, 'Mum would have done it this way', and try to keep my cooking as close to hers as possible. She is amused when I cook for her, and if I ask her to rate my dishes, she laughs and says I am getting close but not there fully yet!

MAKHANI DAL

Ingredients

- 150 gm whole black lentil
- 50 gm red kidney beans
- Salt to taste
- 1 tbs ginger, chopped
- 50 gm butter
- 3 tbs single cream
- 1 tbs oil
- 1 tsp cumin seeds
- 4–5 garlic cloves, chopped
- 1 large onion, chopped
- 1 green chilli, chopped
- 2 medium tomatoes, chopped
- 1 tsp red chilli powder
- 1 tbs coriander powder
- 1 tsp fenugreek powder
- 1 tsp garam masala
- 1 tbs lemon juice

Method

- Soak lentils and kidney beans overnight in 600 ml water.
- Drain and refill fresh water, enough to cover the lentils.

- Cook the lentils with ginger, salt and green chillies. In a pressure cooker it will take 10–12 minutes and in a pan it will take 60–80 minutes. Cook until the lentils are soft.
- Heat oil in a pan and add cumin seeds.
- When they start to crackle, add garlic. Sauté till light brown in colour.
- Add onions and cook until light brown in colour.
- Add chopped tomatoes, coriander powder, red chilli powder, fenugreek powder and garam masala.
- Sauté for a minute and then add chopped tomatoes.
- Cook the mixture for 5–6 minutes until tomatoes are soft. Add the cooked lentils with butter and cream to this mixture and simmer for 12–15 minutes. Adjust the seasoning. Add lemon juice before serving.

MUM'S ALOO MASALA

Ingredients

- 400 gm potatoes, cut into batons
- 1 medium tomato, chopped
- 2 tbs vegetable oil
- 1 tsp nigella seeds
- 1 tsp cumin seeds
- 1/2 tsp ginger, chopped
- 1 green chilli, chopped
- 1 tsp turmeric powder
- 1 tsp coriander powder
- 1/2 tsp red chilli powder
- 1 tsp salt
- 1/4 tsp garam masala
- 1 tbs coriander leaves, chopped
- 1 tsp fenugreek leaves

- 1 tsp mango powder
- 5 gm ginger, julienned

Method

- Heat oil in pan, sauté nigella and cumin seeds, green chilli and ginger.
- Add potatoes, red chilli powder, coriander powder and turmeric. Cook on slow flame for 3 minutes.
- Add chopped tomato and salt. Cover and cook until soft.
- Sprinkle juliennes of ginger, garam masala and chopped coriander leaves, fenugreek leaves, mango powder, and serve hot.

JAMSHEDPURI SPICY OKRA

Ingredients

- 500 gm okra, washed and slit vertically
- 1/4 tsp onion seeds
- 1 tsp turmeric powder
- 1 tbs tamarind pulp
- 2 tsp mustard oil
- 2 tsp mustard seeds, ground into a paste
- 1 tsp chilli powder
- 1/4 tsp sugar
- 1/2 tsp salt

Method

- Heat oil in a wok or pan, add onion seeds, sauté and then add okra, stir.

- Add salt, chilli powder, turmeric powder and sugar. Cook on low heat.
- Once the okra is cooked, add mustard paste mixed with tamarind pulp.
- Sauté for a few minutes, remove and serve hot.
- Note: This dish can be garnished with crisp fried Okra and coriander sprigs.

KESAR–PISTA NAAN KHATAI

Ingredients

- 100 gm plain flour, sieved
- 100 gm semolina, sieved
- 100 gm ghee or unsalted butter
- 100 gm powdered sugar
- 1/2 tsp green cardamom powder
- 1 tbs yoghurt
- 1/4 tsp baking soda
- A few strands of saffron infused in warm milk
- 30 gm pistachio slivers

Method

- Cream the ghee and sugar together.
- Add cardamom powder, yoghurt and baking soda and mix lightly.
- Add saffron milk and pistachio slivers.
- Add flour and semolina and knead to a soft dough.
- Divide into small balls and keep them aside.

- Arrange on a greased baking sheet and bake in a moderately hot oven (300F) for 30–40 minutes.
- Remove, cool and store in an airtight container.

GEETU VERMA, GLOBAL VICE PRESIDENT, MARKETING, FOODS AND REFRESHMENTS, UNILEVER

MOTHER: BINA GIDWANI

I must have been around six years old when Doordarshan showed just one feature film a week and everybody in our apartment building in Chembur, Mumbai, would wait with much excitement for Sunday to arrive. Since we did not have a television at home, I would take my sister, who was three years old then, to go to watch the film at my cousin's house. But one part of me would wait for the news break when we would scramble down the stairs to our home where Mom would be waiting with our Sunday evening treat—an outstanding potato and mutton keema kebab. When I look back, there are so many memories attached to that kebab: of me, the fiercely protective elder sister, taking care of my younger sibling, our secret treat at home, and, more than anything else, of Mom's nurturing ways. She made the mutton keema into cutlets too and we polished them off with bread and chutney within minutes so that we could catch the rest of the movie upstairs.

Mom is frail now and unable to cook as much as she used to but she has trained our domestic help, who has been with us for over thirty years, to make the kebabs so that they remain a part of our occasional special family dinner. Only, the mutton kebab has now made way for all sorts of variations including one with vegetarian keema and even sooran (elephant yam), but for me the magic of Mom's Sunday evening kebab will never fade.

While the first ten years of my life were spent in a joint family where vegetarian dishes were not very popular, the food on our table changed dramatically when my parents moved out to set up our nuclear family, in a small apartment. Suddenly the food became very diverse and we started eating lots of vegetables—turai, karela and greens.

Since she was a working woman, Mom learnt to cook our meals efficiently, saving time but managing to make the food tasty. I remember her cooking in our tiny kitchen, cutting, chopping, grinding, frying, all at the same time to prepare an entire meal for us in just thirty minutes. While other women in the family spent a couple of hours standing by the cooking stove preparing their mutton curries, Mom learnt the fine art of using a pressure cooker to fry the masala, pop in the mutton and pressure cook it so that her signature mutton curry was ready in twenty minutes and as tasty as tasty can be! Her ability to conjure up great quantities of food quickly meant that there was never any panic in our home if guests dropped in, unannounced.

I am glad I picked up Mom's efficient way of cooking. It is such a blessing in Europe where I work and run my home myself, with no domestic help. And when I lived and worked in Delhi, this efficiency helped me invite friends for impromptu dinners, because I too do not panic at the prospect of cooking without prior notice.

My childhood memories of Mom's food are about the everyday stuff she made—her chawal and sai bhaji is one of my favourites from her repertoire. I have eaten this in many Sindhi homes, but I love my mom's sai bhaji the best. This dish tastes different in every home because every family adds different combinations of vegetables and spices.

My mother's Sindhi kadhi used to be the highlight of some Sundays. Mom followed her recipe to a T. It was a medley of methi seeds, curry leaves, drumsticks, brinjal, carrots, potatoes, tamarind, and a little sugar to balance the flavours. We would have the *khatta meetha* kadhi with rice and to complete it there would be sweet boondi sprinkled on top of the rice and roasted papad for a delicious crunch. It was a lot of hard work but Mom would prepare it once every 2–3 weeks.

On Diwali, Mom made her saat subzi, a dish featuring seven vegetables, which she served with puris and sabudana khirni made with thickened milk, sugar and kesar. To this day, my Diwali celebration does not begin without her saat subzi. Despite living in another country, I still make the subzi and call her to tell her so that I feel like I am celebrating Diwali with her.

Even though we had no brothers, my sister and I looked forward to Rakhi because our cousins would come home and we would all crowd around the kitchen stove where aloo tikkis would be fried. We would compete to eat the largest number till the mothers and aunts would groan and point out that more than 150 had already been eaten.

Dad and I loved Mom's seyel bread, a Sindhi special made from leftover bread slices, rotis or pao. She would either make a green coriander masala or pyaaz-tomato masala with lots of spices, and I remember I would soak up the gravy with slices of bread, pao or leftover rotis, and have it with papad.

Hare masalewale bhindi aloo (ladies' finger and potato in green masala) and tayeri (sweet rice made with jaggery) was a family favourite. When I went home the last time, my mother made tayeri and I took a container of it with khatti meethi dal (sweet and sour dal) to my paternal aunt who, at ninety-two, still remembered how my mother would pamper her with it. My aunt passed away a few weeks after our meeting, and I am so glad that I had the opportunity to treat her to Mom's delicious tayeri.

My memories of Mom's food are also, somehow, tied up with our train travels across India. My father was a railway employee and we would travel in quaint first-class coupes on trains back then. We once took a memorable train journey going to our guruji's ashram in Rishikesh and Haridwar. The Frontier Mail took twenty-four hours in those days to reach Delhi, where we stopped for a break before heading to Haridwar and Rishikesh. Mom had made a lot of preparations for the trip. She was carrying this delicious, crispy pyaaz masala roti laden with ghee, which we ate with a dry aloo ki subzi. There was also lots of koki, another Sindhi staple, in both sweet and savoury varieties, that we had with chai, and it was a complete meal in itself. Then there was a big flask of hot milk, which she portioned out to everyone. There is something exciting about sitting by the train window, watching fields and rivers fly by while sipping a hot cup of milk.

There are other food memories that still cause a lump in my throat. My Nani, an incredibly independent woman who lived by herself well into her eighties, would treat us to this simple but spectacular split moong ki khichdi with ghee and whole seeds of cardamom that we ate with turi ki subzi and crushed papad on top. I learnt the recipe from Mom and today, when I crave her food, I reach out for the recipe and cook it for myself. Mom also made a great mutton biryani that was moist, aromatic and full of flavours, and I have never eaten anything like it, ever.

When I moved to Delhi, Mom moved in with us so that the kids had company. On Sundays, the ritual at home was that every member of the family had to cook something. We would all sit around the kitchen table and have an extended brunch where we would catch up on each other's lives. Mom's dish got the maximum attention and she would be thrilled that her grandchildren loved her food. She was always particular that we all sat together and ate. Even as kids, when we moved into our tiny apartment, she insisted that we have a small dining table set up in our drawing room so that we could all eat together. Because of her hospitable and social nature, most of the family parties would be in our home. She would serve delectable fare such as biryani, keema tikki or mutton curry and chawal and everybody would have a blast. Fortunately, I have inherited her ease in the kitchen and find it easy to host impromptu parties and get-togethers.

Mom makes the world's best date rolls, a festive dessert that is famous among friends and family. She cooks dates, walnuts and dry fruits to make this delectable dessert, which is then rolled in a bed of grated coconut, chilled in the fridge and cut into rolls.

She hails from a family where everybody is passionate about cooking. Though she has been incapacitated for the last six months, she was quite active in the kitchen till recently. In fact, going into the kitchen and cooking up something was therapy for her when she was a career woman and my sister and I were still in school. Today I find that cooking is therapy for me too.

SINDHI TAYERI

Ingredients

- 1 cup rice
- 3/4 cup jaggery
- 3 tbs thinly sliced copra
- 3 tbs black raisins
- 1 tbs honey
- 3–4 whole black peppercorns
- 1 cardamom
- 2 tbs ghee
- 1 tsp sugar
- Salt to taste

Method

- Wash and soak rice for 30 minutes in adequate water. Separately, melt the jaggery in 1/2 cup of hot water and keep aside.
- In a pan, heat ghee on medium flame, add sugar, cardamom and black peppercorns and stir.
- As soon as the sugar browns (30 seconds or so), add the soaked and drained rice, add a pinch of salt, and adequate water to half cook the rice. Cook on medium heat.
- Once the water is absorbed, add the jaggery water, cover and simmer till the rice is done and water fully absorbed.
- Once cooked, add 1 tbs of honey for glaze, copra scrapings, black raisins and stir in.
- The tayeri is ready to be served with bhindi aloo subzi and roasted papad. It's great for a weekday or weekend lunch.

SEYAL BHINDI PATATA

Ingredients

- 400 gm okra slit lengthwise but kept whole
- 400 gm patata sliced round
- 1 tsp coriander powder
- 1/2 tsp red chilli powder
- 1/2 tsp jeera powder
- 1 tbs oil
- 1 medium-sized tomato, pureed

Ingredients for the chutney masala

- 1 medium-sized bunch of fresh green coriander leaves
- 2 green chillies
- 6–7 cloves of garlic
- 1-inch piece of ginger
- 1 medium-sized onion

Method

- Finely chop all of the above and grind in a mixer to make green chutney.

Method

- Stir fry the okra and patata in oil in a flat pan. Add the dry spices and salt to taste once the vegetables are golden and cooked. Keep aside in a flat open dish.

- Heat a tsp of oil, add the green chutney masala and cook for 10–15 minutes on slow flame, add the tomato puree, salt to taste and cook for another 10 minutes.
- Once the masala is cooked, pour over the vegetables and serve with the tayeri.

SINDHI ALOO TIKKI

Ingredients

- 5–6 medium-sized boiled and peeled potatoes
- A small bunch of coriander, cleaned and finely chopped
- 2 green chillies, finely chopped
- 3–4 old or new bread slices, soaked in water and instantly removed, squeezed dry
- 1/2 tsp chaat masala
- 1/2 tsp tawa-roasted coriander seeds, coarsely ground
- 1 tsp oil
- Salt to taste

Method

- Mix all the ingredients and make a dough. The consistency should be such that the mix holds together. If it does not, add another 1–2 slices of bread.
- Add oil as needed to scrape off the remnants from the bowl and make it smooth and glazed.
- Form small round tikkis with your hand, keeping your hands oiled to prevent the dough from sticking.
- Heat oil in a pan and deep fry the tikkis. Ensure the oil is of the right temperature. The tikkis will break and soak up too much oil if the oil is not hot enough or burn if oil is too hot.

- Serve with the green chutney.
- If the dough is of the perfect consistency, these tikkis absorb less oil when deep fried than shallow fried.

SABUDANA KHEERNI

Ingredients

- 1 litre whole milk
- 1 medium cup sabudana washed, pre-soaked for half hour and strained
- 3–4 cardamoms coarsely ground
- Few strands of kesar soaked in a tbs of water
- 8–10 pieces each of badam, pista, thinly sliced
- 4–5 tbs sugar or as per preference

Method

- Add all the ingredients (except the nuts) to the milk and cook on slow flame till the milk starts to thicken and takes on a golden hue and thickish consistency.
- Add the nuts and serve, ideally hot.

HARIT NAGPAL, CHIEF OPERATING OFFICER, TATA SKY

MOTHER: PREM NAGPAL

I grew up in Delhi back in the sixties and seventies. Life was simpler than it is today, and most households ate simple, traditional fare. I was a single child, but that certainly did not mean extra pampering in terms of being offered a luxury of choices in food. I grew up on a diet of parathas—not stuffed ones but rotis, with a generous amount of ghee smeared on them. Most days, it would be parathas for breakfast, with ajwain and namak sprinkled on top, before I went to school. In winter, Mummy would serve the same parathas but with the addition of a giant dollop of home-made gajar halwa on top. This is how I learnt very early to appreciate balance and contrasting flavours in food.

We had no live-in domestic help, and so Mummy made no-frills meals: dal-roti was everyday food and non-vegetarian dishes were strictly only for Sundays and holidays. On Sundays, she pampered us with delicious meals. Lunch was mutton with gravy, and I remember soaking up the fiery gravy with the crisp, thin, tawa-fried chapattis she made. This was in itself a treat because during the week, these were made thick in order to save time, and we could only eat about three of them. I remember eating six or seven chapattis every Sunday, because the mutton was yummy and perfect to go with them.

On those Sundays when she was not preparing any heavy non-vegetarian dish, Mummy would pamper us with pooris and heavenly aate ka halwa, and I still don't know a more delicious manner to start the day. It was pure indulgence. When I look back, I am struck by how there was no use of refined oil in those days. Everything was made in ghee and no one worried about cholesterol and calories. Everybody worked hard, the kids walked to school and played in the open, running around till it was time to go home.

Mummy was great with traditional Punjabi food, which she had learnt to cook from her mother. We ate the usual Punjabi staples, such as chana, rajma-chawal, pakodewali kadhi-chawal with roasted dal papads speckled with black pepper. We were not much of a rice-eating family, but when we did have rice, it was always peas pulao, with whole spices. So many decades after leaving Mummy's home, eating this dish—which continues to be my comfort food—fills me with nostalgia.

Her chole, with thick black gravy, was the family favourite. She would be horrified that some families added a bit of tea to their chole to make the gravy dark in colour. Her secret was cooking the chole in an iron kadhai (wok) so that the chole organically turned deep, almost black in colour. Mummy passed away some time ago, but we still have that kadhai in the house. I use it once in a while, when I am in the mood, and cook chole the way she did, remembering her as I cook. I learnt the recipe from her when I was a teenager and remember the arguments we would have because I would make the gravy of my chole thick, because I liked it that way. She would say: '*Paani aur dalo. Itna sookha nahi banta hai chole.*' The fact of the matter, however, was that she did not want me to improvise her recipe.

I remember the time I was living by myself in Delhi and would call her for recipes, because I did not like eating out and preferred to cook my meals. I would reserve Sunday afternoons for ambitious assembly-line cooking; there would be a mutton dish, two types of dals, two subzis being prepped and cooked simultaneously. Mummy would be on call and sometimes direct me live, while the cooking was on. Once done, I would cool and refrigerate the dishes and have great meals during the week.

When my parents came visiting once, I served them the same food Mummy used to cook. Dad relished the meal and remarked that I had prepared Mummy's dishes better than she herself could. She was not amused at all, because for her it was important to follow the recipe as she had been taught. Every time I cooked with her in our kitchen, she controlled me. But when she was not around to lay down the rules, I started adjusting the spices, adding something, leaving out other stuff, and I was happy with the results.

Mummy was not very experimental in her cooking. Rice kheer, with lots of dry fruits, was added to regular food to make it festive. Winter dessert was gajar halwa, made with khoya and brilliant red carrots, the kind not easily available these days. The halwa would be a beautiful pink colour because of the khoya in it. A yellow custard with chunks of banana and apples and strawberry jelly on top was a weekly ritual. We always overate this dessert because it was so different from the usual Punjabi fare.

When the grocer delivered the custard powder and jelly, I would wait with much anticipation for her to make it.

Baisakhi and Lohri were celebrated with enthusiasm. We had lots of rewdi, gajak and moongphali (peanuts), which was great for evenings when you got together with the family and sat around chatting. Gajak and rewdi came from the market, of course, but Mummy made the moongphali with spices and aamchur, and that was a treat.

Mummy's bread pakodas were the best. And so were her palak, onion and aloo pakodas—light, airy and crisp. We Punjabis love our pakodas.

Back in those days, the food that we served guests was simple too. There was no concept of starters before the main meal. Guests were served a spread that featured two to three types of home-style salads—in the form of sliced kheera, gajar, mooli and tamatar sprinkled with aamchur—papad, the main course and two desserts. While the family ate either rice or roti for everyday meals, having guests over meant that there would be both rice and roti.

In our house there was an unusual post-dinner ritual of serving coffee as a special treat when we were entertaining. In those days, we had only just discovered coffee. When we had guests over, it would be my post-dinner task to beat a mix of instant coffee, water and sugar together in a cup till it turned white and frothy. I remember sometimes this would take what seemed like thirty minutes, and my parents would then ask me to beat it some more, to impress the guests. They then divided the frothy mixture into mugs, added hot water and milk. Drinking that foreign import at our house was the high point of the meal.

She was a proud cook. Sometimes, I remember, she would be quite envious if Dad or I admired somebody else's cooking. She would then go about trying to find out why that person's dish was better than hers. Maybe it was because it challenged her primary role—she wanted to be the best feeder of her family.

PINDI CHOLE

Ingredients

- 250 gm kabuli chana
- 5 tbs refined oil
- 3 green chillies
- 2-inch piece of ginger
- 2 tbs coriander powder
- 1 tsp red chilli powder
- 1/2 tsp turmeric powder
- Onion, tomato, coriander leaves—for garnish

For the masala base

- 4 tsp cumin seeds
- 6 cloves
- 5-inch piece of cinnamon
- 6 pcs green cardamom
- 3 pcs black cardamom
- 3 tbs anardana

Method

- Soak the kabuli chana overnight. Pressure-cook with water and a pinch of salt, for 20 minutes.
- Dry roast the whole masalas on low flame for 5 minutes, till the aroma starts to release.
- Fry the ground masalas and keep them aside.

- Heat oil in an iron kadhai. This is the secret of the black gravy, not tea leaves.
- Add slit green chillies and julienned ginger, and fry for 30 seconds.
- Add the ground masala and let it cook for 2 minutes while constantly stirring it. Any more and it will burn.
- Add coriander powder, turmeric powder, red chilli powder and some salt, and cook while stirring for another 3 minutes, or till the mixture darkens.
- Add the boiled chana with its water and keep stirring till the gravy thickens.
- Press the chana with a flat ladle or a pav bhaji maker to break some chanas. This will further thicken the gravy.
- Garnish with raw onion rings, sliced tomato and chopped coriander.
- Serve with bhaturas or layered parathas.

PAKODEWALI PUNJABI KADHI

Ingredients for pakodas

- 150 gm besan
- 1/2 tsp turmeric powder
- 1/4 tsp red chilli powder
- 1/2 tsp garam masala
- A pinch of ajwain
- Salt to taste
- A pinch of baking soda
- 1 large sliced onion
- Fresh coriander leaves
- Refined oil

Ingredients for kadhi

- 1 cup curd, kept overnight at room temperature
- 50 gm besan
- Salt to taste
- 1 tsp garam masala
- 1 tsp turmeric powder
- 1 tsp chilli powder
- A pinch of baking soda
- 30 ml refined oil

Method for pakodas

- Mix all ingredients with water and make the batter.
- Set aside for 30 minutes.
- Deep fry in refined oil. Keep turning the pakodas till they are golden brown.

Method for kadhi

- Mix curd, besan, half spoon each of garam masala, turmeric powder, red chilli, and salt to taste. Your kadhi mix is ready.
- Heat oil in a pan.
- Add cumin seeds, and when they splutter add fenugreek seeds, sliced onions, sliced green chilli and grated ginger.
- Fry for 3–4 minutes.
- Add half teaspoon red chilli powder.
- Now add the kadhi mix prepared earlier.
- Increase heat while stirring, till the mixture comes to a boil.

- If the mixture is thick, add boiling water to make it thinner.
- Cook on low heat for 10 minutes.
- Add the pakodas to the kadhi and cook for 5 more minutes.
- Garnish with sliced onions and coriander leaves.
- Eat it with plain chawal or jeera rice.

ATTA HALWA

Ingredients

- Equal measures of wheat flour, sugar and pure ghee

Method

- Melt the ghee in a heavy-bottomed pan over medium heat.
- Add the flour to the ghee while stirring continuously, and keep stirring till the mixture turns dark. This could take about 8 minutes.
- Boil one cup water on the side and slowly add to this mix.
- Cook while stirring for 2 minutes, till the water gets absorbed by the flour.
- Now add the sugar and continue to stir, and cook for another 3–5 minutes, till the mixture is thick again and the ghee begins to separate from the mixture.
- Garnish with grated almonds or cashews.

HARSHA BHOGLE, SPORTS COMMENTATOR, AUTHOR

MOTHER: SHALINI BHOGLE

A lot of my food memories are about home-style Maharashtrian food that Aai cooked. But she was also very experimental in the kitchen, with the result that the family got to taste a diverse range of dishes, all adapted to our taste.

I grew up on a vibrant, cosmopolitan university campus in Hyderabad, with neighbours from different regions of the country. My brother and I constantly talked about the heavenly aromas that came from the house of our Muslim neighbours, and before long, Aai's curiosity was piqued. One morning, she went over and requested the lady of the house for the recipe, explaining that her sons were enchanted with the aromas from their kitchen. The lady very kindly shared the recipe, and Aai cooked the saalan for us with one big difference: while the original saalan was non-vegetarian, ours became alu saalan or batatyache saalan! It was a hit in our family for a long time.

Aai would make a Maharashtrian-style chinch-gul (tamarind and jaggery) bhendichi bhaaji, the chinch-gul combination being a very Maharashtrian thing. I loved the sweet-and-sour gravy of the bhendi and would enjoy it with hot polis (chapattis).

She also prepared a very distinct palakachi patal bhaaji, a thin gravy dish made from spinach with lots of groundnuts in it, and we would enjoy this with poli or steaming-hot rice. This bhaaji is typically made using alu (colocasia) leaves, but because we had a profusion of leafy vegetables available in Andhra Pradesh, Aai simply adapted the recipe and cooked it with palak.

My grandmother often stayed with us, and when Aai, who taught psychology at the university, got busy with work, Grandma cooked for us. One of her specialities was varan-phala, a flavoursome dal, into which she dropped diamond- or triangle-shaped pieces of the dough used to make rotis. The whole thing would then be boiled together to a thickish consistency and was a delicious meal in itself.

My other favourite is what we called gurutiya bhaat. In those days, when we had fever and loss of appetite, Grandma would make this slightly sticky, overcooked rice, with lots of black pepper powder. We had it with lime pickles and instantly felt better and very hungry!

The other thing Aai made a lot was mudda bhaaji, which was a soft-cooked palak bhaaji with besan and a seasoning of red chillies and garlic. Because my father never liked garlic, while the rest of us did, she would pour the seasoning into our individual plates rather than into the whole bhaaji, so that everyone could enjoy their meal as they liked it.

Since she had a hectic schedule teaching postgraduate students, Aai's cooking was functional, but that did not mean she had no time for the rituals of Indian households. Summers were about making pickles. We bought raw mangoes, which would be chopped into even pieces with a bit of koy (seed) in them.

The mangoes would then be put in *bharnis* (ceramic containers), with salt and oil, and left to marinate for a few days. Once the spices were added and the pickles ready, we enjoyed it for the entire year. Aai would also despatch us to the neighbours' with pickles in steel containers, and we would return home carrying their pickles in our containers! This was the big annual exchange of pickles among households on the campus.

Aai also made delicious puran polis stuffed with a jaggery-and-chana-dal filling. Unlike other households, where puran polis were made only for festive occasions, we had them regularly at home. In those days, the puran had to be hand-churned, with a 'puran yantra', a kitchen gadget in which the stuffing for the puran-poli was ground till we got the right consistency. Aai would serve us the puran-polis with ghee poured over them; my grandma preferred hers soaked in milk.

As kids we would wait for the arrival of Ganpati, because Aai would make khirapat—grated coconut, dried dates and raisins mixed together as an offering for the lord.

Mango season meant daily helpings of aam ras at home. While some families put the mango pulp in blenders to make the ras, Aai would make it with her hands, because she believed ras always tasted better when it was a little lumpy. My grandma would add some milk in the aam ras, along with a spoon of ghee, and it was so tasty that we could have many servings of it.

Another of my favourites is the gud-dani, a home-made chikki that Aai prepared by tossing peanuts into caramelized jaggery and pouring the mix on to a flat plate. You waited for it to dry and only then got to taste the goodness of the gud with the crunch of the peanuts.

Though I never formally learnt any cooking from Aai, I learnt a few things by observing her when I assisted her with her chores, such as making chapattis (but mine always looked like maps of India) or pounding the peanuts to make shengdanyache kut (crushed peanuts).

It has been a while since I last ate a meal cooked by Aai, but when I close my eyes and think of her, I remember her alu saalan and the arbi chi bhaaji, which, if the arbi was not fully cooked, would result in all of us having an itchy throat.

MUDDA BHAAJI

Ingredients

- 1 bunch spinach, chopped coarsely
- 1 cup tur dal
- 3 tbs besan
- 1 lemon-sized ball of tamarind soaked in warm water
- 2 red chillies
- 1/2 tsp mustard seeds
- 4–5 pods of garlic
- 2 tsp oil, for seasoning
- Chilli powder, turmeric powder and salt to taste.

Method

- Cook the spinach in a little water.
- Pressure-cook the tur dal with a little turmeric powder till soft and add to the cooked spinach.

- Extract the pulp from the soaked tamarind.
- Add the besan to the tamarind pulp and make a smooth paste out of it. Add this to the spinach-and-dal mixture and whisk well. Add chilli powder and salt. Boil this mixture again.
- Season with whole red chillies, garlic and mustard.
- This traditional Maharashtrian preparation can be enjoyed both with chapattis and steaming hot rice. Most folks will have this with some home-made ghee poured on top of the rice and a papad on the side.

CHINCHAGULACHI BHENDI

Ingredients

- 250 gm bhendi, cut in two-inch-long pieces slit vertically
- 1 lemon-sized ball of tamarind, soaked and pulp extracted
- Salt, turmeric and chilli powder to taste
- Oil to sauté the bhendi
- 2 tsp powdered jaggery, or as per taste
- 3 tsp roasted groundnut powder, or as per taste
- 1/2 tsp mustard
- A pinch of asafoetida

Method

- Heat oil in a kadhai, splutter mustard and add a pinch of hing.
- Add the bhendi and sauté till it begins to change colour.
- Add tamarind pulp and salt, and boil.
- Add turmeric and chilli powders.

- When the bhendi is cooked, add a little more water, jaggery powder and roasted groundnut powder. The peanut powder will give the bhaaji a nutty flavour and also give it body.
- Switch off the flame after a couple of minutes and garnish with fresh coriander leaves.

HRISHIKESH KANNAN, RADIO JOCKEY, VOICEOVER ARTISTE

MOTHER: RADHA KANNAN

Having left home at the age of seventeen, I spent years in Delhi for my college education but kept going back home to Lucknow for summer holidays. After months of eating insipid, mindlessly made food at the hostel, I would take the Shatabdi Express from Delhi to Lucknow, where Amma would be waiting and the house full of the aromas of avial and all the other stuff that she knew I loved to eat. Later, when I lived alone in Mumbai at the beginning of my career in radio, I would long for the food that Amma cooked for us with such love. For me, the memories of being home will always be synonymous with the aroma of her avial, thogayal and rasam.

I come from a traditional Tam–Bram (Tamil–Brahmin) family, and books and great meals were an inseparable part of my growing-up years. My brother and I did not have the most fashionable clothes in our wardrobe, but for our birthdays or special occasions, such as Pongal or Deepawali, we would each get a good book to read, and Amma would have a special meal for us. Birthdays meant a feast, or sadhya, laid out on a banana leaf, and I still look forward to family occasions, such as a wedding or a naming ceremony, so that I get to eat a great meal on a plantain leaf.

When Amma entered her marital home as a young bride, she discovered right away that the food tradition there was completely different from what she was familiar with. While she is from Kumbakonam town in the Thanjavur district of Tamil Nadu, Dad is from the North Arcot district, and the food cultures in these places are not even remotely common. But she had a friend in her mother-in-law, who taught her a lot of authentic cooking from her side of the family, so that Dad never missed the food he loved. Even after all these years he still prefers to eat the food that he is familiar with, and it is evident in the way our tastes differ. While I love the thakkali rasam (tomato rasam) from Amma's side of the family, Dad loves his molaga rasam (spicy rasam) from his Amma's family. Over the years, Amma has learnt to strike the perfect balance and cater to our individual tastes with practised ease.

I have always been fascinated by the vast variety in south Indian cuisine. To me, the idea that you can have a three-course meal—sambar-rice, rasam-rice and thayir shaadam (curd rice)—all your life is so beautiful. And every day, that meal can be made different by simply replacing one element in the meal. Sometimes the sambar is substituted by an avial or a kootu, which can be made with so many different vegetables, and you feel you have had a great new meal!

I vividly remember some of the meals that Amma would feed us as children. Some days, she would make her trademark vengaya sambar (sambar with pearl onions) or sweet potato sambar with rice, vaazhaka subzi (raw plantain subzi), and I would eat like a glutton. Another day, it would be my favourite thakkali rasam with rice and appalam and a pachadi on the side, and it would be a memorable meal that I would finish off with some thayir shadam.

I must confess that after years of living in Mumbai, setting up a home of my own and eating all sorts of global food, I sometimes find myself searching for Amma's kind of food in restaurants that claim to be 'south Indian', but don't really know the right way to make a sambar or rasam.

Amma also used to make this lip-smacking arbi subzi—beautifully roasted round pieces of colocasia—which is the best accompaniment to rice.

During Janmashtami, Amma had a variety of treats for Lord Krishna, of which my favourite was the sweet appam. She would draw the Lord's feet from the doorway of the house to the *pooja ghar* (prayer room) and make wonderful prasadam, which we got only after it had been offered to the Lord.

Even now, when I go to meet my parents in Whitefield, Bangalore, Amma is disappointed if I suggest we dine out. For her joy lies in getting into her kitchen and cooking up a riot to feed us on our visits to her home.

Amma's mor kozhambu, the south-Indian version of kadhi, minus the besan, goes perfectly with raw banana or cabbage subzi, and the appalams that Paati (grandma) used to make and dry on the terrace during summers. My father used to have aavakkai mango pickle mixed with rice and an appalam crushed into it, and nowadays I find myself giving in to that temptation.

Amma learnt this recipe from Paati who made the best mor kozhambu in the family. Since butter for ghee would be churned at home, there would always be plenty of sour buttermilk available, and so, once a week, Paati would make mor kozhambu. This dish was also made during auspicious occasions and festivals—the first course in a festive meal begins with rice, ghee, paruppu (plain, salted tuvar dal) and mor kozhambu.

Amma is proud of the fact that she now makes Paati's mor kozhambu better than even Paati's own daughters.

Amma's pachadi was another delightful dish that I still adore—my favourite was the one with fresh tomatoes and capsicums in it.

Ours is an extended family of foodies. For Deepawali, we all converged at my paternal uncle's beach house on the way to Mahabalipuram, where we had endless celebrations, mostly centred on food. Pongal was always at my maternal grandmother's house in Delhi. She made the most delicious pongals—sweet and savoury—and taught my mother to make it perfectly. The Pongal tradition in our household continues because my wife, a north Indian, has learnt the secret of the perfect pongal from my mother and prepares it for us.

There is something about the magic of food made at home, and I can see it playing out in my house with my two daughters. I never cease to be surprised by the fact that when my wife and I decide to order some food from a restaurant, my elder daughter prefers to eat a simple thayir sadam made at home. It is the magic, I think, of food made by her mother. It will always be special.

KOOTU

Kootu can be made with a variety of vegetables (spinach, cabbage, snake gourd, bottle gourd) and is a gravy dish.

Ingredients

- 1/2 cup yellow broken moong dal

- 1 cup finely chopped vegetables
- 2 whole red chillies
- A few peppercorns
- 4 tsp split white urad dal
- 1 tsp chana dal
- A pinch of hing/asafoetida
- 4 tsp grated coconut
- Salt to taste

Method

- Cook the moong dal and vegetables together in a pressure cooker or a heavy bottomed pan.
- Dry roast the hing, chillies, pepper, urad dal and chana dal and grind to a paste with the coconut.
- Add the paste and salt to the cooked moong dal and vegetable mixture, and stir nicely till it blends smoothly.
- Garnish with one teaspoon urad dal, browned lightly with curry leaves in a little ghee.

PONGAL

Ingredients

- 1 cup rice
- 3/4 cup split moong dal
- A pinch of hing
- Salt to taste
- 1/2-inch piece of ginger, grated
- 1 tsp peppercorns
- 1 tsp cumin seeds
- 4 tsp ghee

Method

- Cook together the rice, moong dal, hing, salt, grated ginger, peppercorns, jeera and ghee, in a pressure cooker, with a little extra water. Mix thoroughly when cooked.
- Heat two spoons of ghee and roast curry leaves with three spoons of broken cashew nuts till golden brown, and garnish.

GOTSU/GOJJU

Pongal is quite bland by itself. It is this accompanying gravy side dish that makes it special. Can be made using capsicum, green tomato or aubergine.

Ingredients

- 2 tsp oil
- 1 tsp mustard seeds
- 1 cup finely chopped green tomatoes
- A lemon-sized ball of tamarind, soaked.
- A pinch of hing
- 2 tsp rice flour
- Salt to taste

Method

- Heat one teaspoon oil; add hing and mustard seeds. When the mustard seeds splutter, add the finely chopped green tomatoes. Add salt to taste and cook, adding a few spoons of water if necessary. Stir.
- Meanwhile, soak the tamarind in hot water and extract the pulp, adding as much water as required to extract all the sourness.

- When the vegetables are cooked, mash them lightly, add tamarind paste, salt and sambar masala, and boil for a few minutes.
- Thicken by adding two teaspoons of rice flour dissolved in water. Let it boil for a few seconds.

APPAM

Ingredients

- 1 cup jaggery, shaved/powdered
- 1/2 cup maida
- 1/2 cup rice flour
- 1/4 cup wheat flour
- 1/2 tsp cardamom/elaichi powder

Method

- Dissolve the jaggery in warm water, mix well. Add the elaichi powder and the different flours. Blend to a thickish consistency, similar to idli batter.
- Drop into hot oil, the size of small idlis. Deep fry on low heat till golden brown. Drain on tissue paper. Serve hot.

MOR KOZHAMBU

Ingredients

- 1 tsp mustard seeds
- 1 tsp oil
- 250 gm vegetables (white pumpkin/capsicum/okra/colocasia)
- 1 tbs tuvar dal

- 1 tbs chana dal soaked for an hour
- 2 tsp cumin seeds
- 3 tbs grated coconut
- A pinch of hing
- 1/2 tsp methi
- 1 tsp urad dal
- 6–7 green chillies
- 1/2 tsp turmeric powder
- Salt to taste

Method

- Heat the oil and splutter the mustard seeds in it.
- Add the vegetables cut into slightly large cubes, and cook with minimum water and salt.
- Grind to a coarse paste the tuvar dal, soaked chana dal, cumin seeds, grated coconut, plus the hing, methi, urad dal, green chillies, turmeric powder and salt, browned in a little oil.
- Add the paste to the cooked vegetables.
- Add salt to taste and half a spoon of haldi, a little water from rinsing the mixer jar and curry leaves.
- Stir well, then add 4–5 cups of sour buttermilk. Allow it to boil on a small flame, stir and simmer just for a minute.
- Switch off the flame and serve with steamed rice.

RAW BANANA KARAMADU

Ingredients

- 2 raw bananas
- A lemon-sized ball of tamarind
- 1/2 tsp turmeric powder
- Salt to taste

- 1 tsp mustard seeds
- A pinch of asafoetida
- 2 red chillies
- 1 tbs each of coriander seeds, urad dal and chana dal, roasted and ground together coarsely with red chillies
- 1 tbs grated coconut, plus 1 tbs for garnishing
- Curry leaves as per taste
- 3–4 tsp oil

Method

- Cut the raw bananas into semi-circular discs after removing the skin.
- Soak the tamarind in warm water, extract pulp and strain, adding plenty of water, so that the vegetables can be fully covered by the tamarind water.
- Add salt and half spoon of turmeric powder, and cook the plantains with tamarind water. Strain.
- In a kadhai, heat the oil and add a pinch of asafoetida and mustard seeds.
- As they splutter, add the cooked banana pieces. Mix thoroughly and roast for a few minutes.
- Add the ground masala and cook for another two minutes.
- Garnish with curry leaves and grated coconut.

CABBAGE KARAMADU

Vegetables like French beans, cabbage, broad beans, etc., are cooked in south India in a thick curry, to be eaten with rice and sambar or rice and rasam. Since sambar and rasam are spicy, the vegetable is simply boiled with salt, and a simple coconut garnish completes it.

My Amma's cabbage curry was delicious. She would add a teaspoon or two of soaked moong dal to very finely cut cabbage. She would begin with a few spoons of ghee, heated in a kadhai, add mustard seeds, urad dal, brown it, add the cabbage. Keeping the flame high, she would sauté it, add salt and a small quantity of water, sufficient to cook the cabbage. She would keep stirring it. The coconut would be added only after the flame was switched off.

The finished subzi would look raw, like a salad, without any change in colour, and yet melt in the mouth.

IRFAN PATHAN, CRICKETER, COMMENTATOR

MOTHER: SHAMIM BANU PATHAN

The happiest food-related memory from my childhood is that of breakfast. Mornings began with Ammi's hot rotis, smeared with oil, which we would dip into steaming hot chai and relish before heading off to school.

The family was experiencing financial difficulties during those years. My father worked twelve–fourteen hours a day to get a paltry salary of Rs 3500. Having three meals a day was a big deal for us back then, and so this humble breakfast was much anticipated. On some days, Ammi would make a green dhaniya (coriander) and chilli chutney, and we would have it for the next couple of days with our rotis and for dinner, with khichdi.

Carrying lunch to school was a luxury for us. We settled for one *nashta* (snack) daily. If we were lucky, we got pocket money of 50 paise, with which we would buy a samosa or masala aloo from a vendor outside the school. If not, the main meal was dinner, and it would mostly be a vegetable salan and bhindi or tinde ki subzi. Aloo was a regular in our household because it was cheap and also filling, and our meals were often potato subzi with rice and dhaniya chutney.

Ammi was a brilliant cook and used whatever she had in the kitchen to make tasty meals for us. She used to make this delicious subzi, with potatoes, eggplant, methi leaves, fresh green tuvar (pigeon peas) and green chillies, that I can have every single day even today. In fact, I love it so much I requested my wife to teach our chef to make it exactly like Ammi does. When eating it with rice or khichdi, I would add just a couple of spoons of milk on it to make it extra special. That habit persists.

I know everyone thinks that their mother is the best cook in the world, and I believe it too. When I started playing cricket at the age of twelve–thirteen, there would be long hours of practice on the field, and the norm was that the players had to get their own lunch. I remember Ammi would come to the cricket ground carrying delicious green tuvar ki khichdi, with coriander and other masalas in it—and she would feed not just me but a lot of other players who were hungry. She would beam with happiness when they appreciated her khichdi and kindness.

Those were tough days, but Ammi knew that if my brother and I were to see our cricketing dreams fulfilled, we would have to get enough proteins and nutritious food. All she could afford back then was a banana for each of us and milk, which we would buy from a neighbouring dairy because it was cheaper than packaged milk. She gave us curd, and if the milk curdled, she would occasionally make a sweet out of it, with gud, insisting that gud was more nutritious than sugar, but we knew that gud was also cheaper than sugar. She would also treat us to sugarcane juice, which was energy-packed and affordable.

Ammi's biryani was amazing and a rare treat—a luxury for us because we could not afford to buy meat and other ingredients for it. As kids, we would wait for Eid so that we could enjoy her biryani and sheer khurma. Eid was a busy, happy day at home because our relatives would come over to greet us; everybody would eat together and go to the mela to have fun. Ammi would prepare for her feast days in advance, and we kids would help her get the ingredients for the biryani together.

During the 2007 India–Australia series, we were playing a match in Baroda, and Ammi prepared her signature biryani for the team. Twenty-five members of the team relished her biryani that day. To my great surprise, and to Ammi's great delight, Sachin (Tendulkar) expressed his desire to eat the same biryani the next day too. He said that biryani always tastes better the day after it is made. Unfortunately, there was no biryani left from the previous day, but Ammi was more than happy to prepare it for Sachin all over again.

Ammi always made a different biryani for Ramzan and Bakrid. I remember, for Bakrid we would also have mutton chops and mutton curry. Ammi's other speciality, which all of us totally loved, was a methi subzi with keema, which beat the other kinds of keema we had, such as aloo keema. Her other standout dish was drumstick curry with potatoes, or drumsticks with mutton or dal, and each variation was brilliant.

Because of our financial difficulties, we never really had sweets in the house. When we felt like having something sweet, she would make hot rotis, sprinkle sugar on top and tawa fry them, so that the sugar melted and coated the roti with syrup. It was a delicious treat for us kids. When she could afford it, Ammi would occasionally make gulab jamuns or malpuas, but those were rarities.

Those difficult times are now decades behind us, but no matter how much we have progressed and prospered since those days, Ammi's roti, crisp and glistening with oil, continues to be our favourite. Back then, we put oil on the rotis, now we eat them with ghee, but the memories of the family—my brother, sister, parents and I—sitting together and enjoying our nashta, in our simple home, still brings happiness to my heart.

LAMB BIRYANI

Ingredients

- 1 kg basmati rice
- 1 1/2 kg lamb
- 750 gm onion
- 250 gm sour yogurt
- 3 large lemons
- Mint and coriander (handful)
- 100 gm green chillies (depending on how spicy you want the dish to be)
- 1 tsp red chilli powder
- 1 tbs coriander powder
- 1/2 tsp turmeric powder
- 1 tsp whole spices (garam masala)*
- 2 tbs ginger-garlic paste

---

* Whole spices: 5 cloves, 4 slightly crushed cardamom pods, 1 tsp cumin seeds.

Method

- Wash and chop the lamb.
- Heat oil in a pressure cooker, toss in the whole spices and roast the lamb along with ginger-garlic and green chilli paste, red chilli powder, coriander powder, turmeric powder, garam masala and salt.
- When this is well roasted and starts changing colour, pressure cook for four whistles. If you like the lamb to be very tender, a couple of whistles more would be fine.
- Check if the meat is tender and allow it to cool.
- Separately, fry the chopped onions in hot oil till crisp and golden brown to make the birista (fried onion).
- Then add a mixture of 250 gm yogurt and the birista to the lamb gravy along with coriander, mint leaves and lemon juice.
- Place a piece of burning coal in the gravy (add a teaspoon of ghee on the coal and immediately cover the utensil to give it a beautiful, smoked flavour.

Preparing the rice for the biryani

- Wash and soak basmati rice for an hour.
- Parboil rice in 3 litres of water along with 2 tbs salt.
- Strain the rice.
- Add a layer of rice to your non-stick utensil, and then add a layer of mutton gravy. Make a couple more layers.
- Pour the oil left over from frying the birista on the top of the final layer of rice and place a couple of burning coals on it.
- Pour a couple of spoons of ghee or oil on the burning coals and quickly place a lid over it to give the dish a smoky fragrance.
- At this point you may use saffron strands mixed with 3 tbs of milk and pour it on the rice to make it aromatic.

GREEN TUVAR AND METHI SUBZI
WITH BRINJAL AND POTATO

- 1 large bunch of methi (fenugreek) leaves, washed, cleaned and chopped
- 750 gm fresh green tuvar
- 250 gm potatoes, cubed
- 250 gm tomatoes, chopped
- 250 gm small, round, dark-coloured brinjals, chopped
- 50 gm green garlic, chopped (if unavailable, use ordinary garlic pods)
- Green chillies and ginger, as per your preference, chopped
- Coriander leaves for garnishing
- 1 lemon
- 1/2 tsp turmeric powder
- Salt to taste
- 100 gm oil

Method

- Heat oil in a kadhai and add the chopped green garlic, chillies, ginger and garlic. Sauté well, till fragrant.
- Add the chopped baingan, tuvar, potatoes, turmeric powder and salt. Sauté for 5–6 minutes.
- Then add a cup of water, mix well, cover and cook on medium flame till all the vegetables are almost done.
- Then add the chopped tomatoes and methi leaves. Mix well and cook for another 5–6 minutes till the juice of the tomatoes integrates with the rest of the vegetables.
- When ready, the subzi should be dry.
- Garnish with coriander leaves and squeeze lemon juice on top of the dish before serving it with rotis or steamed rice.

KIRAN MANRAL, AUTHOR

MOTHER: SHAMA SHEIKH

When I look back at my childhood, what I remember vividly is Mamma pampering me with hot cups of chicken soup and croutons when I fell ill. To this day, whenever I feel low or unwell, that chicken soup is an instant pick-me-up. And I crave the comfort foods from when I was a little girl. I would curl up in bed with a good book, under my favourite blanket, eating piles of Mamma's crispy French fries. Even today, French fries with ketchup and potato chops—mince-filled potatoes dipped in egg and fried—are comfort foods that I can have any amount of. Strangely enough, cold khichdi eaten from the fridge is also one of my comfort foods!

I have many childhood memories of Mamma in the kitchen, cooking up amazing meals, because Dad was a foodie and loved entertaining. Sometimes the guests would arrive at breakfast and still be around at dinner time, and Mamma would still be serving food with a smile.

She was a fabulous cook. An east Indian Catholic married to a Muslim, she taught herself to cook all the dishes that he loved, with the result that the food in our house was a fusion of both cultures.

Since my father loved good food, even a regular meal at home would be a spread: a meat-based dish, fish fry or curry or prawns, a vegetable dish, raita and rotis. When I think of Mamma's cooking, the dishes that have stayed with me are her drumstick dal, which I crave; her methi aloo that nobody can ever match; and her turai and bhindi subzis that I can have copious amounts of.

When Dad passed away suddenly, Mamma's cooking simply went on the back burner as our survival took precedence. She started working long hours in a bank and returned home tired. So our weekday meals became just khichdi, which I ate cold, right out of the fridge, when I returned from school. I remember now how hard she tried to make our weekend meals interesting, endlessly taking down recipes from television cookery shows and preparing them for us on Sundays.

Our favourite dishes for Sunday lunch would be a fiery chicken curry, masoor dal pulao, a methi or bhindi subzi, and for dessert it would be custard with jelly, coconut cake or just a simple vanilla cake. Mamma was passionate about cooking and put all of herself into it on weekends. And because I was already a foodie, I soon became a plump, happy child.

When Dad was alive, Mamma would pull out all the stops on festive days and prepare either mutton or chicken biryani, dal gosht, peas pulao and keema kebabs, served with raitas and chutneys on the side. Because he loved all things sweet, dessert was always in multiples—there would be caramel custard, phirni, semiya and kheer. The sweet tooth that I developed in my childhood has followed me into my adult life, and a meal is incomplete for me if there is no dessert at the end of it.

Mamma makes the best prawn pulao and biryani ever, but as she gets older, it is getting difficult for her to make these too often, and so these treats are now limited to occasions like birthdays, anniversaries or Christmas.

I sometimes wonder if watching her prepare endless meals for guests—the penalty one pays for being a good cook—is the reason I have an aversion to cooking. As a young woman, I thought being a good cook would mean I would end up having no time or life for myself. Though I am able to make a decent meal when I put my mind to it, I think, in retrospect, I should have learnt some of her culinary skills. But I believe her culinary skills have passed on to my son who enjoys the process of cooking and creating dishes, even though he does not get into the kitchen too often.

POTATO CHOPS

Ingredients

* 300 gm chicken or mutton, minced
* 750 gm potatoes
* 3 big onions
* 7–8 green chillies
* 10–12 pods of garlic
* 1 1/2-inch piece of ginger
* 1/2 tsp pepper powder, or to taste
* 1/2 tsp each of jeera and elaichi powder
* 1 tsp garam masala powder, or to taste
* Juice of 1 lemon
* 1/2 tsp turmeric powder
* 2 whole eggs, whisked well
* Salt to taste

Method

* Boil potatoes with a little salt; peel when cold, mash and keep aside.

- For the stuffing, finely chop onions, green chillies, ginger and garlic.
- Put a pan on the fire, add oil, and then add onions, chillies and garlic. Cook till soft.
- Then add the mince and cook for 10 minutes.
- Now add the powder masalas and turmeric. Mix well, till the mince is coated with the masalas and soaking it up.
- Add salt and a little water if required and cook well. Add the coriander leaves and lemon juice. Mix well again.
- Take a portion of mashed potatoes in the palm of your hand.
- Make a bowl shape, fill a portion of the mince mixture into it, close the edges to form a ball and gently flatten into a patty. Repeat to make several patties.
- Cover the patties with breadcrumbs, dip them into beaten whole eggs and deep-fry.
- Serve with green chutney or tomato ketchup.

PRAWN PULAO

Ingredients

- 500 gm prawns, cleaned
- 400 gm basmati rice
- 2 tbs ginger and garlic paste
- 2–3 green chillies, sliced
- 3 ripe tomatoes, chopped
- 3 big onions, chopped
- 1 tsp garam masala
- 2 tsp red chicken or mutton masala (Mamma swears by Sarvajanik red masala that comes in a bottle)
- Chilli powder, as per taste

- 1 soup cube for flavour
- Coriander leaves to garnish
- Oil of choice
- Salt to tase

Method

- Wash, drain and marinate the prawns with salt, lemon juice, chilli powder and red masala.
- Wash and soak the rice for 15–20 minutes.
- Keep the pan on fire, add oil and fry the chopped onions till they are pinkish in colour.
- Add ginger-garlic paste till aromatic, then add tomatoes till they are well fried and mashed into the onion and ginger-garlic mixture and garam masala.
- Now add the marinated prawns and fry in the mixture till well coated. Add the rice and fry till all the ingredients are well integrated and the rice is coated with the masala.
- In the meantime, boil water (double the amount of rice being used), add the soup cube and rice.
- Add the juice of half a lemon, stir and cook on a slow fire till the rice is cooked.
- Garnish with chopped coriander, sliced green chillies and a dash of lime before serving.

KUBBRA SAIT, ACTOR

MOTHER: YASMIN SAIT

A long time ago, somebody once looked at my mother's palm and told her: '*Aap Annapurna ho, aapke ghar se koi bhooka nahi jayega*', and it has been always like that. Sometimes both of us walk into an empty restaurant and it fills up magically within minutes. I know it sounds weird but I have seen it too many times to not believe it.

I left home for my studies and work a long time ago but, even today, when she visits me in Mumbai, Mumma makes my favourites—mutton biryani, bagare baingan, and kachumber with tomato, cucumber, onion, green chillies.

Mumma has always been the provider of delicious food but the one dish that my entire family hungers for is her mutton biryani. The maternal side of our family in Mysore has this one signature dish—aloo ghosht ka salan—which Mumma says her mother used to cook for the family every single day. Of course, there were other things to accompany it, such as methi keema, but the aloo ghosht had to be made fresh every day. Mumma says a visitor to their home who stayed for a couple of days carried back the tale that our family ate the same salan for days together! The funny thing is that Mumma continues to make the aloo ghosht ka salan for us. I love it best with a little mango chutney, made by my ammi (grandma), squished into it.

Growing up at our family home in Bangalore, Mumma cooked simple, everyday fare but there would always be lots of things on the table—rice, salan, salad, a vegetable preparation and rotis. I remember being a fussy eater as a child and driving Mumma to tears because I would sit at the dining table for hours, dawdling over the food without eating a morsel. But, she says, I more than made up for it when I hit my teens and developed a huge appetite. In fact, she now calls me the 'man of the house' because I am the only one who notices and critiques her food, pointing out if there is an imbalance among the various components in a dish.

Over the last decade or so, I have become quite the foodie and an ardent fan of Mumma's cooking. I love the simplest things she makes, such as her khichda—I can have loads of it at any time. Mumma also makes a delicious dal with drumsticks and raw mango and a simple beetroot aloo salan that can lift a blah kind of day and make it sunny.

Because I notice the minutest detail about whatever I eat, I would often compare Mumma's dishes with the ones made by Ammi. For example, as a child I compared Mumma's Maggi with Ammi's and insisted that Mumma's was not a patch on the one Ammi made. Also, that Ammi's tomato rice, spicy, moist and flavoursome, was much better than Mumma's. But I adored the bagare aloo that Mumma made as an accompaniment to the tomato rice. The aloo would be crisp on the outside and soft inside. The crunch would add excitement to the soft tomato rice. On festivals, when the rest of the family relished her sheer kurma, Mumma always made sure I got my own special dessert, mutanjan, because I never liked sheer kurma.

When I was a kid, my grandfather would often say, '*Aaj kal ke bachchey bahut kamjor hain kyonki khatey nahi hain* [Children these days are weak because they don't eat well].' Aba would sit with us kids when we ate and would crush the rotis that Mumma brought to the table, straight off the tawa, and we would eat them with eggs, keema, dal or bheja—some of the things that she cooked for breakfast. It would all be so delicious that we would eat five rotis each without realizing after fussing about eating one!

When my friends know she is visiting me in Mumbai, they invite themselves to a biryani meal. The last time she was home with me she prepared biryani for 100 people, waking up at dawn and preparing the meal in the basement of the building. The party started at noon and wound up after midnight when the guests left, carrying some of the biryani home. Mumma's biryani is on my list of things to learn but I am sure I will never be able to achieve what she does with this dish.

MUTTON/CHICKEN BIRYANI

Ingredients

- 1 kg basmati rice
- 2 1/2 kg chicken or mutton (approximate portion size of chicken is 125 gm, mutton portion size 100 gm)
- 1/2 litre oil
- 1 kg onion sliced lengthwise
- 12–15 cloves
- 6 pieces cinnamon
- 200 gm ginger paste
- 100 gm garlic paste
- 4 gm thick curd
- 3 tsp chilli powder

- 1 tsp turmeric powder
- Salt to taste
- 1 kg medium-sized potatoes, peeled
- 3 medium-sized tomatoes chopped in two halves
- 8–10 green chillies, with just the heads chopped off
- 1 big bunch coriander leaves, cleaned and chopped finely
- 1/2 cup mint cleaned, but not chopped

Method

- Use a big vessel to cook; the bigger the vessel, the better so that there is space to mix the rice and masalas with the chicken or mutton.
- Heat oil in the vessel, add cloves and cinnamon. In a few seconds, add the sliced onions.
- Fry the onions until translucent. Add ginger and garlic pastes and keep stirring, ensuring it does not stick to the bottom of the vessel and burn.
- Now add the chicken/mutton and mix well. Once the meat starts to cook, it will release water. Keep stirring and add chilli powder, turmeric powder and salt.
- Add the thick curd and let the meat cook in the spices. Monitor to see how much water the meat releases and add just enough water to cook the meat.
- Meanwhile, in a separate vessel, boil the peeled potatoes with some salt.
- Once the meat is tender, add the boiled potatoes whole, tomatoes, green chillies, coriander and mint leaves to the biryani khorma and leave it to blend with all the other ingredients in the vessel.
- As the biryani khorma is getting ready, get a vessel of water boiling. Simultaneously soak the rice in room temperature

Cricketer and sports analyst Ajit Agarkar says his mother makes the tastiest vegetarian meals. Seen here with his mother, Meena Agarkar, wife, Fatima Ghadially, and sister, Manik Agarkar.

A young Ajit with his doting mom, Meena Agarkar.

Credit: Amish Tripathi

Author Amish Tripathi says he learnt precious life lessons from his mother, Usha Tripathi, through the way she cooked and fed her children.

Credit: Anavila Misra

Designer Anavila Misra is learning how to cook wholesome meals for her son from her mother, Urmil Sindhu. She is seen here with her mother and father, Dr Jagveer Singh Sindhu.

Credit: Anupam Banerjee

Michelin-starred chef Anupam Banerjee, director of food and beverage, The St. Regis Beijing, says he learnt how to cook with love in his restaurants from seeing his mother and grandmother cook with abundant love for their families.

Credit: Anuraag Bhatnagar

Anuraag Bhatnagar, chief operating officer, The Leela Palaces, Hotels and Resorts, says his mother, Urmila Bhatnagar, inspires him every day.

Film-maker Ashwini Iyer Tiwari with her mother, Lata Iyer, who has also been her partner in several culinary adventures.

Ashwini Iyer Tiwari's mother, Lata Iyer, and aunt, Geeta Balan, have her eating out of their hands with their sumptuous cooking.

Artist Atul Dodiya craves the simple Kathiawadi food his mother, Nandkuvar Dodiya, pampered him with in his childhood.

London-based Michelin-starred chef Atul Kochhar says popular dishes in his restaurants are often inspired by the food his mother cooked for him as a child.

Atul Kochhar says his mother Sudesh Kochhar's dal preparations are often his inspiration for the popular offerings on the menu at his London restaurants.

Geetu Verma, global vice president, marketing, foods and refreshments, Unilever, says her working mother Bina Gidwani's efficient, organized manner of cooking inspires her in her own kitchen and at the workplace too.

Tata Sky CEO Harit Nagpal's mother, Prem Nagpal, initiated him into the culinary world by supervising his cooking and giving him tips.

Cricket commentator and author Harsha Bhogle grew up on his mother's home-cooked food, often inspired by the various cultural influences in their neighbourhood in Hyderabad.

Hrishikesh Kannan, radio jockey and voiceover artiste, says his mother Radha Kannan's festive sadhya meals are the high points of his life. Seen here with his mom and father, V. Kannan.

Cricketer and commentator Irfan Pathan recalls the time when the Indian cricket team, including Sachin Tendulkar, feasted on his mother's biryani when they were in Baroda for a match.

Kiran Manral, author, says her mother, Shama Sheikh, took time off from her hectic work schedule to cook up delightful dishes for their weekend meals.

Kiran Manral, author, with her mother, Shama Sheikh, and son, Krish Shaikh, who is now a teenager and often tries his hand at cooking.

Actor Kubbra Sait says her mother Yasmin Sait's memorable biryani lunches at home are a magnet for her friends in Mumbai.

Kubbra Sait with her mother, Yasmin Sait.

Manisha Girotra, chief executive officer, Moelis India, still remembers her mother Promila Girotra's versatility in the kitchen.

The Girotras enjoying a family meal.

Manisha Girotra with her mother, Promila Girotra, and daughter, Tara Agarwal.

Manu Pillai, author and historian, says his mother, Pushpa Pillai, cooked up meals that were inspired by the cuisines of different states of the country. Seen here with his mom and sister, Indrani.

India's Olympic medal-winning boxer Mary Kom remembers watching her mother, Akham Kom, cook modest but delicious meals with herbs and vegetables from their tiny garden and fish caught from the nearby pond.

Meeran Chadha Borwankar, former commissioner of police, Pune, says her mother, Shunny Chadha, made her childhood memorable with incredibly versatile cooking and her multiple talents in other spheres of life.

Meeran Chadha Borwankar with her mother, Shunny Chadha.

Cricketer Mithali Raj with her mother, Leela Raj, and niece, Anagha Raj.

Actor Nikhat Khan Hegde (top right, in white kurta) says her mother Zeenat Hussain's Eid meals have always brought the family together to share happy moments. Seen here with her ammi, sister, Farhat Khan, and brothers, Faisal Khan and Aamir Khan.

Nikhat Khan Hegde (in green kurta) with her ammi, Zeenat Hussain, brother, actor Aamir Khan, and sister, Farhat Khan.

Sambit Bal, editor-in-chief, ESPNcricinfo, with his mother, Saswati Bal, whose dishes he now tries to replicate for his family.

Sambit Bal says his early exposure to the culinary world was from watching his mother and grandmother, Manorama Dhal, cook in their kitchen in Orissa. He still craves those farm-to-table meals.

Sandip Soparrkar, dancer, choreographer and actor, says his mother, Rani Soparrkar, taught him to fend for himself in the kitchen and keep a good home.

Satyen V. Kothari, founder and CEO of Cube, a fintech company, remembers the delicious masoor dal and pav meals, and treat days with pizza made by his mother, Neena. Seen here with his mom, father, Vijay Kothari, and daughter, Zoe Kothari.

Satyen V. Kothari's mother, Neena Kothari.

Author Shanta Gokhale loved the Konkanastha Brahmin meals her mother, Indira Ghokhale, cooked for the family. She still remembers the modaks and chaklis she prepared.

Author Shanta Gokhale with her mother, Indira Ghokhale.

Shashi Tharoor, MP and author, craves the malakushyams, upperis and mezhukkuvarattis that his mother, Sulekha 'Lily' Tharoor, cooked for the family. Seen here with his mother and sisters, Shobha and Smitha.

Shashi Tharoor sharing a fond moment with his mom, whose feisty spirit he adores.

Radio jockey Shonali Rohan Ranade says she learnt the rudiments of cooking by helping her mother, Kalpana Madhukar Joshi, in the kitchen.

Sudha Menon, author, with her mother, Pramila Radhakrishnan, whose home-cooked food inspired this book. From her, she learnt that one can cook the most delicious meals with the humblest ingredients if they are cooked with love and generosity.

Sudha Menon with her mother, Pramila Radhakrishnan, sister, Sangeeta Menon, and niece, Aarya Menon.

Actor Suhasini Maniratnam says her mother Komalam's food has her drooling even today.

Suhasini Maniratnam with her mother, Komalam Charuhasan, and cousin, actor Anu Hasan.

Actor Tisca Chopra says her mother Pammi Arora's lotus stem with besan is the stuff that she dreams of. Seen here with her mother and daughter, Tara.

Actor Vidya Balan says her mother Saraswathy Balan's adai, dosas and molagapodi are comfort foods that she craves.

Vidya Balan with her mother, Saraswathy Balan.

V.R. Ferose, senior vice president and head, SAP Academy for Engineering, says his mother Fathima Rasheed's vegetarian curries and desserts make him drool. Seen here with his mother, father, V.A. Rasheed, and brother, V.R. Riyad.

water for ten minutes and then add it to the boiling water with some salt. When the rice is al dente, drain the water and keep aside.

* Remove the oil from the biryani khorma in a bowl, set aside some of the chicken/mutton in a dish. Layer the rice and pour some khorma over it; repeat the layers and finally pour the oil reserved from the khorma on top and keep the vessel on the gas until the biryani is steamed.

* At this point, cover the vessel with a flat lid with hot water. Keep the flame on high, occasionally lifting the lid to check if the steam is rising to the top of the vessel.

* Gently stir the rice from side to side and bottom up to mix and blend the rice well with the khorma. so its mixed well.

* Lower the flame and simmer it for a few minutes, then switch off the gas. Don't open the vessel for at least 10 minutes so that the steam stays within for some time.

* Always ensure each serving gets a portion of the meat, aloo and rice.

KACHUMBER SALAD

Ingredients

* 3–4 big onions, finely chopped
* 3 big tomatoes, finely chopped
* 2 cucumbers, finely chopped
* 3 green chillies, finely chopped
* 1/2 cup coriander leaves, finely chopped
* 1/4 cup mint leaves, finely chopped
* 4 gm thick curd
* Salt to taste

Method

* Soak finely chopped onions in a bowl of cold water and wash them. Drain.
* Mix the finely chopped tomatoes, cucumbers, green chillies, coriander and mint leaves with the onions. Toss this into the thick, beaten curd, add salt and serve with biryani.

BAGARA BAINGAN

Ingredients

* 1 kg purple, round, uniform-sized brinjals, with 4 lengthwise slits
* 150 ml oil
* 3 finely chopped onions
* 3 tsp garlic paste
* 500 gm tomatoes pureed
* Curry leaves for seasoning
* 1/4 tsp mustard seeds
* 2 tsp chilli powder
* 1/4 tsp turmeric powder
* Lemon-sized ball of tamarind, washed, soaked in water and pulped
* Salt to taste

Method

* Heat oil in a vessel, add the curry leaves and mustard seeds. Once the mustard seeds splutter, add chopped onions and fry until it starts to brown. Add garlic paste and stir.

- Add chilli powder, turmeric powder and cumin powder and fry for a few seconds.
- Add tomato puree and cook until the tomatoes are done.
- Now add brinjals and mix well with the masala, add salt, cook for a bit until the brinjals change colour, then add tamarind pulp.
- Let it cook until the brinjal is soft and leave it on simmer till the oil starts separating.
- Serve with biryani and kachumber.

MUTTON ALOO METHI GRAVY

Ingredients

- 1/2 kg tender mutton
- 4 medium-sized potatoes, peeled and cut into halves
- 75 ml oil
- 1 large onion, finely chopped
- 1/2 cup fenugreek leaves, finely chopped
- 1 tsp ginger paste
- 1/2 tsp garlic paste
- 3 medium-sized tomatoes, pureed
- 3 tsp grated coconut, ground into a fine paste
- 1 1/2 tsp chilli powder
- 1/4 tsp turmeric powder
- 1 tsp coriander powder

Method

- Heat oil in a cooker, add chopped onions and cook for a few minutes.
- Then add ginger and garlic paste and fry together.

- Add chilli powder, turmeric and coriander powder. Stir well for a couple of minutes and then add tomato puree, cooking it till the oil separates.
- Add methi leaves, mutton and potato to this and fry until the aroma of roasted methi is strong and the oil separates.
- Pour water into the cooker, add coconut to make a consistent gravy and pressure cook 10–12 minutes until the mutton is tender. Turn off the gas, and allow the preparation to stand for 15–20 minutes.
- Serve hot with white rice and cucumber, tomato and onion kachumbar on the side.

MANISHA GIROTRA, CHIEF EXECUTIVE OFFICER, MOELIS INDIA

MOTHER: PROMILA GIROTRA

There was this vanilla cake that my mother would bake for me when I was a schoolgoing kid back in Shimla where I grew up. It was a simple, no-frills cake that she would bake in an old oven by the time my brother and I returned from school at 4 p.m. That was the best thing about coming home: rushing into the kitchen, grabbing the cake tin, slicing a big chunk of the cake and feeling my teeth sink into that slice of heaven.

Even today, while travelling in any part of the world, the aroma of a vanilla cake wafting out of a coffee shop or patisserie brings my world to a stop, and I am transported back to the dining table in our home in the hills, where we would chat with Mom about school and eat up all the cake!

I was born in a middle-class family in Chandigarh. My father worked in a public-sector bank and my mother was a mathematician who taught in a college. Later, we accompanied my father on a posting to Shimla where my mother took up a job in a school.

What I remember from those times was the remarkable ease with which Mom would manage both her career and the house. Dad loved socializing and every evening we would have about a dozen people for dinner at our home. Shimla was a small town back then and there was little to do in the evenings by way of entertainment and, so, families believed in getting together over food and conversations about politics, sports and current affairs. Food on our table for these occasions would be a mix of Himachali, Kashmiri and Punjabi cuisines—we are Punjabi but our friends were Himachali and Kashmiri. Mom would make a diverse range of traditional Indian dishes such as aloo gobhi, gajar mutter, gajar ka halwa, palak paneer, laal paneer, rajma, chilka dal, and so on. I always looked forward to lunch on Sundays because Mom made my favourites—rajma chawal, palak paneer, chicken curry and vanilla ice cream.

I think Mom's food was so delicious because she was committed to making our meals mindfully. She had an extensive repertoire, ranging from the regular bharwa bhindi to paneer kofta, cakes, pizzas and gulab jamun. My brother and I had memorable birthdays with Mom making pizza, pasta, burgers, cheese sandwiches and cakes, in addition to Indian snacks such as aloo tikkis. Our friends would talk about the food for days after our birthday parties , and I must confess it made me rather proud to hear so much praise for Mom's cooking.

I studied at Loretto Convent School in Shimla where we were only allowed to carry food that would not dirty or stain the floor. For the 10 a.m. break, therefore, we would have a tomato or egg sandwich with biscuits and lunch would be chapatti–bhaji rolls because those were non-messy and easy to eat.

My mom was one among three daughters and had learnt everything about cooking from her mother, my grandma. A vegetarian, she started cooking non-vegetarian food only after she married my father.

Though a working woman, Mom always found time to pamper us with a variety of snacks, of which I distinctly remember the kheer-puri, spicy potato nuggets, cheese balls, salads, chilli cheese toast, fried idli, and sabudana and potato cutlets. My favourites were her aloo parathas and egg sandwiches with mustard sauce that made my school tiffin very exciting.

Mom is a great believer in the rejuvenating qualities of home-made dal–chawl. Back when we were kids, a steaming plate of dal-chawal was her solution for all sorts of health problems—whether we had fever, cold, stomach ache or bruises from a fall, we would be fed yellow tur dal-chawal with dahi and tucked into bed. Miraculously, we would be well the next day.

HOMESTYLE CHICKEN MASALA

Ingredients

- 750 gm to 1 kg chicken, cut into 8 pieces
- 1/2 cup curd
- 2 tbs ghee
- 1 black cardamom
- 3 green cardamoms
- 1-inch piece of cinnamon
- 1 bay leaf
- 2–3 black peppercorns
- 2 large onions finely chopped
- 2 tbs ginger-garlic paste
- 2 tsp red chilli powder
- 1 tbs coriander powder
- 1/4 tsp turmeric powder

- 1 cup yoghurt, whisked
- 3–4 ripe tomatoes, pureed
- 1 tsp garam masala powder
- Salt as preferred
- 1-inch piece of ginger, julienned
- Kasuri methi for garnishing
- A handful of coriander leaves, finely chopped for garnishing

Method

- Marinate the chicken pieces in a mixture of curd, half the ginger-garlic paste, some salt, turmeric, red chilli powder, and let it rest for at least 2 hours.
- Heat the ghee and oil and add the whole spices. Cook for 2 minutes.
- Now add the chopped onions and sauté till translucent and pink.
- Add the remaining ginger-garlic paste and sauté for 2 minutes.
- Add red chilli powder, turmeric powder, coriander powder, garam masala powder, salt and sauté for 2 minutes.
- Now add tomato puree and sauté well till it blends with the masala.
- Now add the chicken and cook on high flame for 10 minutes, stirring occasionally.
- Lower the flame and add the remaining curd, then add 2 cups of boiling water, cover with a lid and cook on a low flame for another 10 to 15 minutes or till the chicken is tender.
- Adjust the salt, now add kasuri methi and garnish with ginger juliennes and chopped coriander leaves.
- Serve with rotis or hot steamed rice.

MY MOTHER'S TAKE ON DUM ALOO

Ingredients

- 500 gm medium-sized potatoes (pahadi variety is the best)
- 2 small sticks of cinnamon
- 2 large cardamoms
- 2 green cardamoms
- 1 bay leaf
- 3 cloves
- 1/2 tsp cumin seeds
- 1 1/2 tsp Kashmiri red chilli powder
- 1/2 cup curd, well beaten
- 3 tsp of fennel powder
- 1/2 tsp dry ginger powder
- 1/2 tsp garam masala
- Salt as preferred
- Oil for frying

Method

- Boil the potatoes till they are tender. When cool, peel them and pierce them all over with a toothpick so that the masala can be absorbed during the cooking process.
- Now deep fry the whole potatoes in hot oil.
- Next, put oil in a cooker, preferably mustard oil.
- Add cumin seeds, and when they start to splutter, add the cinnamon, cardamom, cloves, bay leaf.
- Lower the flame and add the Kashmiri red chilli powder.
- Stir quickly and add the potatoes, sauté for a minute.
- Now add the beaten curd to it.

- Simmer for a couple of minutes till the curd turns into a nice red colour.
- Now add fennel, ginger powder and garam masala. Stir well.
- Add a glass of water, stir well, add salt to taste and pressure cook for just one whistle, then let it simmer for 5 minutes.
- Open the cooker when cool.
- The dum aloo is ready to be enjoyed with rotis, naan or even jeera rice.

Tip: To get the potatoes just the right consistency for the dum aloo, add them to the pan of water when it is warm and allow the water to boil. After 2 minutes of boiling, switch off the flame, cover the pan and let the potatoes be in the water for 15–20 minutes. This will prevent the potatoes from overcooking and crumbling when pierced.

MANU PILLAI, AUTHOR, HISTORIAN

MOTHER: PUSHPA PILLAI

As a child I would eat everything from kanji and chammandi (rice gruel and chutney) to keema parathas and chole bhature. It was only as an adult I realized how privileged I was to have enjoyed so much variety

An ordinary day would include naan and something delicious with it in the morning (yes, for breakfast!), and then a paratha with interesting stuffing ranging from cabbage to chicken or paneer for lunch at school. Dinner was strictly Malayali—rice, at least two curries, and what we call thoran or mizhakkuvarati.

The rice too was of two types and we used to call them 'fat rice' and 'thin rice'. There was variety in the fish preparations too. I only liked fried fish, but did eat curry once in a while if it was 'Christian fish curry' i.e. as prepared by our Malayali Christian friends, who omitted certain ingredients, with the result that the taste was very special.

The mizhakkuvarati was a special delight; any vegetable made that way is delicious to eat, both with rice and chapatti. Vendakka (okra) was a favourite, but also brinjal, beans and other greens. It is one of those rare dishes that is quick and easy to make but utterly delicious to consume. In fact, it often happened that we would love it so much that we would ask for more, only to find that it was over because very little had been prepared in the first place. This was not a bad thing, because the memory of the taste would linger and the next time a mizhakkuvarati was made, it would go down even more wonderfully. After all, a lot is in one's head.

From the start, everybody at home had different tastes, all of which were cheerfully accommodated. I am baffled as to how Mummy managed it because it was not as though she was at home all day, cooking. Achu (my father) was a vegetarian, and he needed Kerala food almost daily; my sister and I had another set of things we liked; and Mummy had her own preferences and a great desire to experiment and do new things. I think we all got to eat what we liked because she thoroughly enjoyed the process of cooking.

Even now, when I proactively ask that we eat more simply, there is inevitably variety on the plate. This may be because of Aandyamichi's (my maternal grandmother) influence. She grew up in one of those old *tharavads* (ancestral homes) in Kerala and, as she herself admits, lived in considerable privilege, with the result that she has very high expectations when it comes to food. If something does not *look* all right on her plate, half the battle is lost. Then each item must add up in terms of taste, and you can read on her face at once what she thinks of the food. It is not the best of habits, but the result is that several generations in our family, while not 'foodies' in terms of eating, do try and make an effort to get the taste right.

My sister is as gifted as my mother, and I too have surprised myself with my culinary skills, though not on a regular basis. And as a rule, though we do have assistance during the day, at least one meal is prepared by a family member, and you can tell the difference. I, for instance, swear by my mother's chapattis. It is difficult to describe, but the outside has a flaky thin crispy texture, and the inside is soft, and that makes it absolutely amazing to scoop up a steaming subzi and chew with delight. The chapattis made by the cook, however, are more regular, and the kind one gets anywhere. They are perfectly edible, but lack that special quality that distinguishes home-cooked food.

Sweets were not a major part of our daily life, oddly enough. On special occasions, such as our naal-birthdays (birthday as per the Hindu calendar), there would be payasam, as also for Onam, Vishu and other festivals. But mostly chocolates or cakes were purchased from outside for dessert, but this was not a routine affair at all. In Kerala, there was a lot more on offer unlike Pune where we lived. There were all kinds of appams, including elayappam, made in a banana leaf; a thick but gooey dish made of jackfruit (I hated it); fried sugary items, and so on.

But that said, if thrown a challenge, my mother could make fairly exotic desserts. Once, when it was difficult to find cake and I expressed a desire for a slice, she surprised me with steamed cake made at home. Except that, given the circumstances, it was made in the idli mould, so that each 'slice' of cake was basically a sweet, delicious idli!

VENDAKKA MIZHAKKUVARATTI

Ingredients

- 250 gm tender okra
- 2 tbs coconut oil

- 1/2 tsp cumin seeds
- 3–4 cloves of garlic, crushed
- 1 tsp coriander powder
- A pinch of turmeric powder
- 1 tsp chilli powder (or as per preference)
- Salt to taste

Method

- Wash and pat dry the okra and cut them into one-inch pieces.
- Heat 2 tbs of coconut oil in a wok or a frying pan.
- Add cumin seeds and when they start to splutter, add 3–4 cloves of crushed garlic.
- Sauté until it turns fragrant.
- Put the okra in and stir until coated in oil.
- Spread it in the pan and leave it alone till the stickiness vanishes.
- Don't stir too much as this causes the vegetable to get stickier.
- Add turmeric powder and coriander powder.
- Add a little of the spicy chilli powder.
- Add salt and stir without crushing the okra.
- Leave the pan on simmer, and occasionally stir the okra again, adding a little more oil, if needed.
- Once done, move the okra—nice and soft, and coated with the masala—to a pretty dish. You can add simple boiled rice to the wok or pan to scoop up all the masala sticking to it. That rice is delicious!

MAMPOO CHAMMANDI

This is a simple side dish to go with hot rice. This chammandi is better made on a grinding stone (ammikallu) in the traditional way.

Ingredients

- 1 cup freshly grated coconut
- 1 whole dried red chilli
- Salt (to taste)
- Tamarind to taste (in my mother's words 'rolled to the size of a small gooseberry')
- 1 small Madras onion
- 1 stalk of curry leaves
- 1 tbs of fresh maampoo or mango blossoms. The blossoms should be fully open—closed ones are bitter—and they need to be plucked, washed, and measured into 1 tbs.

Method

- Roughly grind salt, tamarind and red chilli together in the small chutney bowl of the mixer.
- Add coconut and mango blossoms to the mixer bowl, and mix gently with a spoon. Grind again, making sure it remains coarse and doesn't turn into a smooth paste.
- Add Madras onion, curry leaves and again use a spoon to mix. Grind it some more.
- Adjust the salt and chilli as per your preference.
- Eat with rice.

Tip: This chammandi can also be converted into a pachadi. Skip the tamarind and follow the rest of the process. Stir in 3 to 5 tbs of not-very-sour dahi. Alongside, make a tadka of 1 tbs of coconut oil. Add in a pinch of mustard and splutter. Break a red chilli into 3 to 4 pieces and drop them into the hot oil. Add curry leaves, fry until fragrant. Pour over the yogurt mix. Your pachadi is ready!

Three generations of women in the family—grandmother, mother and sister—have contributed to the writing of this recipe, given that this was something my great grandmother used to make many years ago.

MARY KOM, BOXING CHAMPION

MOTHER: AKHAM KOM

I was born in Kangathei, a tiny village around 60 km from Imphal. My parents were landless labourers and the food we ate at home was very simple, modest fare. But even so, I sometimes find myself thinking of those meals with my family, in our tiny mud house with its thatched roof.

My parents worked hard in the fields of landowners in order to earn a living and feed their four children. Since I was the eldest, I began working in the fields when I was just a little girl so that I could help them support the family.

One of my favourite things to eat as a child was kangshoi or chamthong (in Manipuri, we just prefix the name of the vegetable that is used in the dish). This was made of fresh mustard leaves and potatoes from our garden or the nearby fields, stewed with fish that came from the local Loktak lake, all boiled together and flavoured with sliced onions, cloves, salt, garlic, maroi (winter leeks) and a bit of ginger. We had the piping hot stew with rice, and I still remember its aroma and the distinct flavours from the herbs that Anu, my mother, tossed into the bubbling pot.

Like other village homes, we too had a patch of garden where my parents grew an array of vegetables—mustard, cabbage, potatoes, tomatoes, garlic, ginger, peas, beans, brinjal, ladies' finger, coriander, and a variety of indigenous herbs such as maroi napaakpi (hooker chives), maroi naakuppi (Chinese chives). Since we were poor, my parents also sold the fresh vegetables in the local market to make both ends meet.

I remember looking forward to our Sunday lunches. City folks will probably never know the value or concept of eating local and seasonal, but in the village, we ate what the earth produced during the changing seasons. This meant the taste and flavour of the food was incomparable. After a week of relentless hard work in the fields, my parents and the four of us would sit down to enjoy a humble but delicious fare: steamed rice, which was a must, along with boot—a steaming hot stew bursting with the flavours of fresh vegetables, dried fish and meat. Meat was a rarity—we couldn't afford it—and would be reserved for special meals. My absolute favourite from the Sunday meal was shingju, a mixture of several greens such as shingju leaves, chopped cabbage, banana or lotus stem, banana flowers, shallots, aromatic roots, herbs such as coriander, ginger, chilli, and fermented fish. Sometimes we ate this as a snack too, and it was very satisfying after a day at school or in the fields.

There are other heart-warming memories of my childhood. Life was hard but also a happy time spent with my siblings. Often, I would be in the kitchen helping Anu with the cooking so that I could lighten her burden. I loved to hang around the kitchen when she made ooti, a traditional dish made with local spices, dried peas, fresh greens and baking soda. At home we replaced the peas with rice, added bamboo shoots, greens and baking soda.

Another of my favourites was a dish of rice, steamed with fresh, soft maize. Though this was considered poor people's food, the taste was matchless. It still takes me back to my childhood and brings back memories of waiting expectantly for Anu to serve this for lunch or dinner! My mother also made spicy chutneys using indigenous greens and herbs, some of them tart and tangy, to which she added fermented fish and served with our meals. Ngari and ngathu were the two fermented fish varieties we used a lot in our home.

Since our family had very limited means, there was not much Anu could do to give us fancy food, and yet, she did manage the occasional treat, using her resourcefulness to prepare something that would have us slurping and asking for more! One of my favourite snacks from childhood was tan, a Manipuri breakfast staple, very much like a puri, that she made with sticky rice flour. I remember it went very well with piping hot black tea. Sometimes she served it with a spicy aloo kangmet, potatoes being a family favourite.

I left home in 2014 and shifted to Imphal, but I still miss the simplicity of life back in my village. When I look back, I realize how lucky we were to be able to eat fresh, organic produce, grown in our backyard. Sometimes I miss tending to that patch of garden and picking fresh veggies for our meal.

I learnt how to make many of the traditional dishes by being with Anu in the kitchen, and I am happy I am able to cook those meals for my family—husband and three sons—today. What makes me happier is that they too love the simplicity of the food from our village and our culture.

AHTRAM KANGSHOI

Ingredients

◆   1 bunch of mustard leaves

- 1 tsp crushed ginger
- 1 tsp crushed garlic
- 3–4 chillies or as preferred
- 2 medium-sized onions, sliced
- 2 medium-sized potatoes, sliced
- 4–5 pieces of fermented fish, or as per preference
- Coriander or other herbs, as preferred (optional)
- Salt to taste

Method

- Wash the bunch of mustard leaves thoroughly.
- Boil a cup of water (or depending upon the quantity of greens) in a pot. Once boiled, add 1 tsp of crushed ginger, chillies, the sliced onions and fermented fish (optional).
- Then add the sliced potato. Cover and cook it for 5 to 7 minutes.
- Add 4 to 5 pieces of fish (depending upon the size of fish and as per preference; in case of dried meat, it has to be precooked until soft), and cook it for another 3 to 5 minutes.
- When the potato is soft, mash half the potatoes in order to give the stew a nice consistency. Then add 1/4 tsp of salt and the mustard leaves torn into small pieces.
- After cooking for another 5 minutes, lower the flame; add 1 tsp crushed garlic (it can also be added in the beginning, along with ginger and onion). You can also add coriander and other herbs for preferred flavour/aroma.
- Cover the pot and leave it for a couple of minutes on a low flame and your curry is ready. (Make sure it is not overcooked and the green of the leaves don't change colour and become dull. The same procedure can be used for other greens as well.)

KOPI BOOT

Kopi means to boil. Boiling vegetables is one of the simplest ways of cooking, but not something that is appreciated in other parts of our country. I chose to give this recipe because it is one of the healthiest foods there is. (The same procedure in this recipe can be followed for other vegetables as well.)

Ingredients

- 250 gm sliced cabbage (you can add carrots, beans or other veggies for additional flavour and taste)
- Salt to taste
- 500 ml water
- Couple of onions, thickly sliced
- Any herb of choice (optional)

Method

- Boil 500 ml of water in a pot/pan.
- When the water is boiled/hot, add a pinch of salt followed by 250 gm sliced cabbage.
- Boil this for 10–15 minutes, making sure the veggies are not overcooked (less water or soup is recommended for better taste).
- Always add the hard veggies first. Thus, if you want to go for a combination of beans, carrot, cabbage or broccoli, beans have to go first as they will take more time to cook.
- It is also your choice whether you want to add other herbs or onions but I prefer to add only salt for taste.
- This is served as an accompaniment with a meal of rice, kangshoi, chutney, etc.

MEERAN CHADHA BORWANKAR, FORMER COMMISSIONER OF POLICE, PUNE

MOTHER: SHUNNY CHADHA

I will always remember the luxury of Sunday morning breakfast back in the day, when I was growing up with my three siblings. Sundays were special because we were allowed to ditch the weekday ritual of fried eggs and toast and have eggs in whatever form we pleased. The additional bonus was that Mom would allow us to have breakfast anytime and anywhere around the house. So, I would indulge in cheese omelette with buttered toast in my favourite corner of the house, with a good book for company. Sometimes it would be Mom's savoury French toast with tomatoes, green chillies and coriander or her absolutely decadent sweet French toast.

Growing up in small towns such as Fazilka, Ferozpur and Faridkot, where Dad was posted as a senior police officer, it was a different life for us kids because other families were wary of police families and would not send their kids to play with us. Our government accommodation was outside the main town, so my siblings and I had to keep ourselves entertained.

Later, Dad shifted us to Jalandhar so that we could get good college education.

Mom was a multifaceted woman who kept a great home, and also sewed and knitted, for which she subscribed to *Women and Home* magazine. She was an instinctive cook and specialized in Continental food, which she was very fond of. But because she had a variety of interests, she trained a cook to take on the daily cooking, preferring, instead, to cook when she was entertaining or for special family celebrations. Baking and making English puddings have always been her forte. Later in life, when microwaves arrived in most households, she started baking in them, and the cakes would be equally scrumptious.

Mom was a teacher for five years before she got married, and has always been very strict with us, especially about nutrition, hygiene and studies. We could not leave home to play till we finished our homework. Sleep time was 8 p.m. sharp. I remember she would sing us the nursery rhyme 'Wee Willie Winkie went to the town, upstairs and downstairs, in his night gown', and the ritual would end with her switching on the bedside lamp and leaving the room. None of us dared to leave the bedroom after that even if we had guests over for dinner!

Like most Punjabi families, we usually had rajma chawal for lunch on Sunday. Occasionally, she would make chicken curry and Punjabi kadhi with pakoda or her exceptionally good peas or yakhani pulao, but my all-time favourite was her delicious tomato kadhi, that I still enjoy making for myself, with steamed rice.

Mom treated us often to tasty snacks. While initially I loved her egg rolls, fragrant with fresh mint, I shifted loyalties when she learnt how to make cheese balls that I loved to pop into my mouth, piping hot.

Mom being a dessert lover, there were always sweet things to eat at home. While the entire family loved her kheer, she would also make seasonal dessert treats for us such as the melt-in-the-mouth gajarela or gajar ka halwa with creamy milk, ghee and dry fruits. Her custards and caramel bread puddings were always a treat and an inseparable part of our school-going years. The one dessert that stood out was her snow pudding, a creation so beautiful and tasty that it kept us all hooked for years.

Mom loved baking and would spend hours patiently baking cakes for the family even though ovens were not as modern and user-friendly as they are now. The problem was that our levels of patience did not match with hers. We would wait patiently for her to finish baking so that we could bite into the heavenly slices but she would refuse, insisting that we wait for Dad to arrive and cut the cake. The wait seemed endless for us because Dad kept late hours, but she would not budge from her stance that he would cut the cake. I still remember, the four of us would wait with bated breath, looking longingly at a baked cake or a snow pudding, but not permitted to even touch it till Dad got home. It taught us that we had to be patient and wait for the good things in life. When we talk about cakes, I can never forget how excited we would be when our birthdays were around the corner because Mom did the most attractive and tasty icing on our birthday cakes.

When I think back about what made her food so tasty, I am now sure it was the way she delicately used spices and herbs such as mint and green chillies in her dishes—just enough to add aroma and heat but not so much that it overpowered the original taste of the dish.

I am not considered a great cook in my family, but I did learn how to make a few of her desserts and the signature Punjabi masala made of onion, tomato, garlic and ginger, that is the base for all Punjabi curries. I am glad I did that because both my boys enjoy my rudimentary cooking and appreciate the meals that I cook for them.

MUTTON YAKHANI PULAO

Ingredients

* 500 gm long-grained basmati rice
* 500 gm mutton chops
* 3 tbs oil
* 2 big onions, thickly cut in long slices
* 6 pods of garlic, chopped
* 1-inch piece of ginger, julienned
* 6 cloves
* 2 badi elaichi
* 8–10 black peppercorns
* 2 bay leaves
* 1/2 tsp turmeric
* Salt and red chilli powder as per taste
* Mint leaves for garnishing

Method

* Clean and wash mutton chops thoroughly.
* Clean and soak basmati rice in water for half an hour before cooking. Keep it aside.
* In a heavy-bottomed pan, heat oil and add onions, garlic and ginger. Just as onions turn pink in colour, add the mutton chops.
* Add salt, turmeric powder, red chilli powder, bay leaves, badi elaichi, black peppercorns and cloves and cook for

about 5 to 7 minutes (don't add water at this stage, as washed mutton will give out its own juices).

♦ Mutton should be 'roasted' well till it is completely coated with the spices and the room is full of the aroma of spices and mutton.

♦ Now add water amounting to 3 times the quantity of rice. Cover and cook on medium flame for about 20 minutes till the meat is well done and one third of the water evaporates.

♦ Add the soaked rice, salt to taste and cover again. After the first boil, lower the flame to medium and continue cooking till the rice settles. It will take 5 to 7 minutes.

♦ Now put a 'tawa' under the pan and bring the heat to minimum. Put a heavy utensil on the lid so that steam does not escape. After about 10 minutes, check to ensure the rice is well cooked. Unlike biryani, mutton yakhani pulao is softer and less oily .

♦ Put off the gas, but do not open the pan for another 5 minutes.

♦ Before serving, garnish the pulao with mint leaves.

TOMATO KADHI

Ingredients for kadhi

♦ 500 gm tomatoes
♦ 1 tbs besan
♦ Hing
♦ 1/2 tsp jeera
♦ Salt as preferred

- 1 tsp coriander powder
- 1 tsp red chilli powder
- 2–3 green chillies or as per spice level preferred
- Coriander leaves for garnish

Ingredients for pakodas

- 6 tbs besan
- 1/2 tsp of red chilli powder
- 80–100 gm water
- 1 small onion, cut into small pieces
- Oil for frying
- Salt to taste

Method

- Wash and parboil tomatoes. Peel them once they have cooled down. Do not throw away the water. It has to be used for the kadhi.
- Put tomatoes in a mixer/blender and make a medium thick puree using the same water the tomatoes were boiled in. When cold, add 1 tbs of besan and mix well.
- Keep it aside.
- Beat water and besan to medium consistency. When dropped in water, besan should float.
- Add chopped onions, chilli powder and salt.
- Deep fry the pakodas till golden brown, take them out and place them on a tissue paper so that it soaks the extra oil.
- Now take out the excess oil, leaving only 2 tbs of oil in the kadhai.
- In the hot oil, add hing, jeera and green chillies.

- When jeera starts to splutter, add the tomato puree and besan mix. Stir continuously so that the mixture does not have lumps.
- Add coriander powder and red chilli powder. Stir continuously.
- When it thickens and comes to a boil, add the pakodas and let them cook in tomato puree for about three minutes.
- Garnish with fresh green coriander leaves and serve with plain hot rice.

SNOW PUDDING

Ingredients

- 1 litre full cream milk (100 gm to be kept separate, without heating)
- 2 eggs
- 4 tbs sugar
- 1 tbs custard powder, yellow or pink in colour

Method

- Break the eggs in a bowl and separate egg whites from the yolks.
- Beat the whites with a fork/egg beater, till fluffy.
- Boil 900 gm of milk and sugar in a wide, heavy-bottomed kadhai.
- Lower the heat and drop a spoonful of the well-beaten egg whites into the kadhai and let it float on the boiled milk.
- Flip it, cooking both sides, and take it out after about 2 minutes.

- Add a second batch of egg whites to the same kadhai of milk and cook similarly for about 2 minutes.
- There should be around 8 egg-white floats. Having soaked milk, they become big and heavy. Keep them side.
- Now lower the flame or even switch it off for some time.
- Beat the egg yolks till they become smooth. Keep them aside.
- Put 1 tbs of custard powder in the 100 gm of cold milk kept separately and mix properly.
- Gently and slowly, add the beaten egg yolk and custard powder mix to the boiled milk in the kadhai. Keep the heat to minimum so that the milk does not curdle.
- Spooning and mixing is very important at this stage or the custard can get stuck to the bottom of the pan.
- When the custard becomes smooth and has boiled well (about 3 minutes), lower the 'fried' egg whites into it. Put off the gas after a minute.
- Now the egg whites will float on the yellow or pink custard.
- Gently pour the custard and floating whites into the bowl you wish to serve it in. A longish bowl/tray would be ideal as more 'snow' can be seen.
- Chill in the fridge for minimum 2 hours before serving. This dessert is a visual treat and was a big part of my happy childhood.

MITHALI RAJ, CRICKETER

MOTHER: LEELA RAJ

I was in New Zealand for the Women's World Cup in 2002, when I was diagnosed with typhoid and hospitalized. I was just nineteen years old then.

I still remember how traumatic it was to be in isolation in an alien country, without my family around. I was lonely and lost, because even my coach and manager were not around and it was terrifying.

I remember waves of homesickness would overcome me, especially at night, and I would weep, thinking about my family and how good it would be to just go home.

One night I went to bed miserable and dreamt I was at home and that Mummy was making my favourite fish fry. The dream was so real that I could actually smell the fish frying and feel it in my mouth but like all good things, this too ended. I woke up and discovered that I was still in the hospital and the fish fry meal was just a dream!

I was never too fond of food. Since I was a child, my attitude was you eat to stay healthy and it is a task that you have to do every day. But over the last two decades, as I travelled across the world playing cricket tournaments and spending long periods of time away, I discovered that the familiar food you eat at home is all about comfort and the love with which it is made. While on my travels to other countries, I often find myself craving the spicy food that I eat at home, but it is not easily available there. The first thing I do when the team packs up is call Mummy and tell her to have my fish fry or mutton curry ready by the time I reach home!

The amazing thing is that Mummy is a vegetarian who has never eaten meat but makes the tastiest non-vegetarian dishes. In fact, she learnt how to cook non-vegetarian food when I started playing cricket as a little girl and the coach told her I needed to eat fish and chicken for protein to build my stamina. Gradually, my brother and father too started enjoying non-vegetarian dishes, but my brother recently turned vegetarian again. The joke in the family is that now my father has to wait for me to return to get a non-vegetarian meal; Mummy simply won't cook it for him alone.

Among my top favourites from her vast list of dishes is a fiery red chilli and coconut chutney that she makes to accompany dosa and idli. I have tried the same chutney in a number of south Indian tiffin places but nothing compares to the taste of what Mummy makes. My friends and teammates love it and request her to prepare it when they visit. In fact, some of them who live in Delhi and Lucknow have taken the recipe from Mummy. Mummy herself learnt the recipe from my paternal grandmother.

Before she got married, Mummy belonged to a family where the women did not spend too much time in the kitchen but focused on their education and other interests. Later, she became a part of my father's Mudaliar joint family where everybody contributed in the kitchen, and so, she never really learnt how to cook. It was only when my parents moved out to set up our home that she learnt how to cook. It was difficult for her, especially the part where she had to cook non-vegetarian food for me. Being a vegetarian, she couldn't even taste the food herself. But she mastered it, and soon became adept at making three to four variants of each vegetarian and non-vegetarian dish so that her kids didn't get bored of the food.

When it comes to great food, there are two festivals I particularly look forward to—Ganesh Chaturthi and Krishna Janmashtami—because Mummy makes sweets that I really enjoy, even though she reduces the amount of sugar so that my diet does not go off track. In fact, I argue with her about this, saying a sweet dish is not a sweet dish if there is no sugar in it.

Mummy's puran poli is something I can overdose on anytime. These are not the kind of polis available in Maharashtra and Gujarat, but much thicker and are stuffed with a preparation of jaggery.

Mummy always packs her puran polis for me when I have to travel by train for tournaments. I eat the polis for dinner while I am away, missing home and her food. In fact, I consider her puran polis my lucky charm and never leave home without a stash of it in my bag.

I also adore the sweet puris she makes for us—she fries the puris and sprinkles powdered sugar on them as soon as they are out of the kadhai. Heavenly!

For Krishna Janmashtami, she makes five to six dishes, some sweet and some savoury, and after the pooja is done in the evening, we get to enjoy all of them. My favourite is her semiya payasam.

When it comes to everyday food, my favourite is her dal palak, tasty and nutritious. I like that the palak is not mashed and pasty like it is in restaurants. I like her preparation of palak paneer because I like some crunch in my food. My idea of a great meal is a portion of rice, dal palak and ghee on top.

I now look forward to the familiarity of Mummy's food. When we toured the West Indies last year, I found the food very bland, even when we ordered from an Indian restaurant. I would get really depressed seeing the food; this is normal because we are away from home for long periods of time and miss the familiar taste of home-cooked meals. On the way back home, I called Mummy from the UK, where we had a stopover, and requested her to prepare something which would be soothing to the eyes as well as to the taste buds. She understood exactly what I meant and when I walked into my house, I was welcomed by the aromas of my favourite fish fry and mutton curry.

Thank God for mothers and the food they cook for us.

FISH FRY

Ingredients

- 1 kg fish (murrel) cut into approximately 16 pieces
- 3 tsp chilli powder
- 3 tsp ginger-garlic paste
- 1 ½ tsp turmeric powder
- Salt to taste
- Oil for frying the fish, as required

Ingredients for marinade (ground into a paste)

- 2 small tomatoes, sliced
- 1 small onion, sliced
- 1 bunch coriander leaves

* Few sprigs of curry leaves
* 1 tsp coriander seeds
* 2 green chillies
* 2 tsp tamarind pulp/white vinegar

Method

* Thoroughly wash the fish pieces in salt and turmeric water.
* Grind the ingredients for the marinade into a fine paste.
* To this paste, add chilli powder, ginger-garlic paste, salt and turmeric powder.
* Mix well and marinate the fish in it, making sure the fish pieces are thoroughly coated with the marinade. Set aside for an hour.
* Now fry the slices in batches of 2–3 pieces in a pan, adding oil as required.

COCONUT CHUTNEY

Ingredients

* 200 gm fresh coconut pieces
* 9 red chillies
* 9 cloves of garlic
* 3 tsp of oil of your choice to pour over the chutney
* Salt to taste

Method

* Grind all the ingredients to a coarse paste in a mixer.
* Take it out in a small bowl and pour the oil. Mix well before serving.

SEA CRAB CURRY

Ingredients

* 6 crabs, chopped in halves and legs separated
* 1-inch piece ginger
* 6–8 cloves of garlic
* Half a lemon
* Coriander leaves for garnishing
* 50–60 ml oil of choice for sauteing the masala
* Milk of one coconut, extracted

Ingredients to be roasted and ground to a paste

* 1 small onion
* 12 green chillies
* 2 tsp coriander seeds
* 2 tsp cumin seeds
* Salt to taste

Method

* Wash the crab pieces and legs in salt water and keep them aside.
* Heat the oil in a pan, add the onion slices and fry for a couple of minutes.
* Add the paste of the ginger and garlic and sauté for 3 minutes till it turns brown.
* Now add the crab pieces and legs and sauté for a couple of minutes.
* Add the prepared masala paste along with salt as per taste and a cup of water.
* Let it simmer for 8–10 minutes.

- Add the coconut milk and cook on a low flame for a few more minutes.
- Turn off the flame when the curry turns aromatic.
- Squeeze the juice of half a lemon and garnish with coriander leaves.

NIKHAT KHAN HEGDE, ACTOR

MOTHER: ZEENAT HUSSAIN

My memory of my growing up years will always be about meal times when our large family—headed by Ammi's phuphi (paternal aunt), including my parents and the four of us siblings—ate together at the dining table laden with a variety of food. Ammi's phuphi was a terrific cook who pampered us with her repertoire of authentic recipes from Benares with the result that we all grew up to be foodies.

Every meal in our home was special, and we ate like every day was a festival. Both Ammi and Grandma believed that food was a source of joy and brought the family together, and they pampered us with food cooked with dollops of love.

The one thing that was unique about our meals was the way they incorporated vegetables into them. There would always be a non-vegetarian dish with either potato, okra or beetroot in it. And there would always be dal and subzi and roti on the table, which we all enjoyed, especially Ammi's parathas, which were so scrumptious that we would have them just by themselves or with seekh kebabs.

While we never thought about it when we were kids, I remember now how the entire family was besotted with

Ammi's cooking. Ammi's family was from Benares while Dad's family came from Shahbad. By the time she married my father, she had honed her culinary skills and immediately won her mother-in-law—our dadi—over with her mastery over food. Our childhood and teenage years are replete with memories of happy occasions when food brought us together. Our home was the place where the entire family—Dad's brother, his sisters and their families—converged for reunions or special occasions.

Ammi was at her best on Eid because all of us looked forward to the traditional Uttar Pradesh recipes that she would lay out for the festive meal. The entire household would bustle with activity on the day of Eid. Abba Jaan and my brothers would go for namaz, and by the time they returned, we women would be all dressed up in our new clothes and looking forward to a hearty breakfast of pooris and kebabs. Preparations for Ammi's seekh kebab would begin from early morning, and till date, she continues to make it the traditional way, over a coal fire. Her parathas would be extra special that day and would be finger-licking good with the korma and kebabs. The highlights of the Eid meal, every year, would be shaami kebab, mutton korma and biryani.

The visitors would start dropping in from around noon, and Ammi would make sure the dining table was full of delectable treats. Since Abba Jaan was a film producer, there would always be a sprinkling of scriptwriters, directors or a couple of actors from whichever movie he was producing at that point. Later, when Aamir bhai (actor Aamir Khan) became a star, his friends and colleagues would come home to celebrate with us. That tradition continues to this day— Ammi knows he will call around mid-morning to say a dozen of his friends will drop by for lunch. He offers to bring some food from outside, but Ammi loves to cook up her special Eid meals.

Ammi also makes the most delicious sweets. As kids we would wait for shab-e-raat when there would be a variety of halwas prepared for the evening meal. Ammi and Grandma would spend the entire day labouring in the kitchen, making moong dal and chane ka halwa, nariyal ki barfi which was Phuphi's special dish, among other things. When it was ready by late evening, I would be given the task of delivering the halwa to the extended family, who lived in the vicinity and waited with great excitement for Ammi's halwa to arrive! Ammi still makes the halwas and each time I eat them, I am transported right back to my childhood.

ZEENAT HUSSAIN (MOTHER TO NIKHAT, AAMIR, FAISAL AND FARHAT KHAN)

I was born in Benares, where I learnt the ropes of cooking under the watchful eye of my paternal aunt, Phuphi Jaan. She was a large-hearted single woman who took my sister and me under her wings after our Ammi passed away when I was just over two years old.

Phuphi was a phenomenal cook, and I learnt everything that I cook today by simply observing her in our kitchen. Katthar ki tarkari was one of her memorable dishes that I managed to learn and is a favourite with the family. Her shaami kebab was my favourite as a little girl, and I am so glad I learnt it because my children and grandchildren now wait for me to make it on special family occasions. She was also a perfectionist. Often, I would offer to help her when there was a *daawat* at home, and she would shoo me out saying I was not yet good enough to cook with her!

When I was eight, Phuphi Jaan took us to Bombay to live with her elder sister and her twelve children, who lived in a sprawling house by the sea in Mahim. It was a period of adventure and discovery as we integrated with our cousins, enjoying an easy camaraderie with them. And while our cousins went off to school in the morning, we were homeschooled since our father was not comfortable with us going to school.

In 1956, a few years after Partition, the entire family shifted to Karachi. But I did not take to my new life there, and two years and much convincing later, Phupi Jaan took us back to our beloved Benares to pick up the threads of our life all over again. A few months later, we returned to Bombay, this time to stay with our chacha (paternal uncle) and his family.

A year later, a chance conversation between Chachi and the sister of my to-be husband, Taher Hussain, led to the two families meeting and the latter asking for my hand in marriage. The marriage took place a few months later, on 25 October 1961. My husband and I then moved to a small one-bedroom apartment on Carter Road, eventually moving to a larger apartment in Pali Hill, as he made his mark in the film industry.

At my in-laws' place, my mother-in-law would love the traditional UP recipes that I would prepare. My arvi ghosht was a favourite with her even though she had her own recipe for it. While I cooked the arvi along with the ghosht, she preferred to peel and cook it separately and add it to the meat later. She loved my interpretation of the dish so much that every time I made it, a portion would go to her house. My brother-in-law (film-maker Nasir Hussain) loved my cooking and would often wait for me to send lunch over to their place. I remember cooking up innumerable treats for my kids and the extended family who loved my koftas, kebabs, biryanis, and the famed aloo subzi of Benares.

The king of halwas in our household is the chana dal ka halwa, which is made by roasting chana in equal amount of ghee and sugar and garnishing it with the choicest dry fruits. It is a laborious dessert to prepare and often my arms ache from all the roasting but everybody waits for me to prepare it on shab-e-barat. This is Aamir's favourite halwa. I have now trained Aamir's cook to prepare the dish so that it is available anytime he craves it. He does not know that I now prepare batches of the halwa and freeze it, so that it can be produced on demand!

Although I don't cook as much as I used to earlier, I make sure I cook on Eid because the children look forward to relishing my biryanis and kebabs. I know for sure that Aamir will call in the morning saying he will come over with ten to fifteen guests to have my biryani. He always offers to order some food from outside, so that I don't have to exert myself, but I love cooking and there is no need ever to order food from outside to feed my kids.

Food does not have to be elaborate to be enjoyed. It simply has to be cooked with mindfulness and love.

CHANA DAL KA HALWA

Ingredients

- 500 gm chana dal
- 500 gm ghee
- 500 gm sugar
- 1 litre milk
- Saffron and kewra to taste

Method

- Wash the chana dal properly and cook it in milk to which a cup of water has been added in order to make sure the dal cooks well.
- Cook till the dal is soft and the mixture becomes dry.
- Put the dry mixture in the mixer and grind it to a smooth paste.
- In a heavy-bottomed vessel, copper if possible, pour ghee and add the finely ground chana dal.
- Stir continuously to roast the ground dal mixture till it turns brown and fragrant, taking care to see that it does not burn.
- After it turns brown, add sugar and roast again till it melts and is fully absorbed. Remove from the stove or the halwa will harden.
- Add saffron soaked in a spoonful of water/milk to the halwa. I love the fragrance of kewra which reminds me of the food back in Benares. I always add a few drops of it to the halwa.

AMMI'S SHAAMI KEBAB

Ingredients

- 1 kg keema
- 200 gm chana dal
- 2 onions cut into big pieces
- 7 whole red chillies
- 2-inch piece of ginger, chopped
- 5 pieces badi elaichi
- 7 cloves

- Black peppercorns to taste
- Salt to taste
- Onion, finely chopped
- Half a bunch of coriander leaves, finely chopped
- Mint leaves as per taste, finely chopped
- A few green chillies, finely chopped
- 1 egg
- Oil to fry

Method

- Wash the chana dal and cook it along with the keema and all the ingredients listed above. Do not use too much water.
- When the dal is fully cooked and tender and the water has evaporated, grind it into a fine paste in the mixer, adding only a sprinkle of water if needed.
- Once ground, add the finely chopped onions, ginger, coriander, mint leaves and green chillies to the mixture and mix it well. Break an egg and add it to the finely ground dal, mixing well to bind the entire thing.
- Make round tikkis of this mixture on the palm of your hands. Shallow fry them till the tikkis are brown on both sides.
- My children and grandchildren love eating this either as a snack or with plain parathas or rotis.

CHUKANDAR GOSHT

Ingredients

- 500 gm mutton, cut into medium pieces
- 500 gm beetroot, finely chopped

- 1 onion, chopped finely
- 1 1/2 tsp ginger paste
- 1 1/2 tsp garlic paste
- 2 tsp coriander powder or as per preference
- 1 tsp red chilli powder
- 1/4 tsp of turmeric powder for colour
- 2 badi elaichis
- 3–4 cloves
- 8–10 black pepper
- 2 big sized tomatoes, chopped
- Salt to taste
- 4 large tbs oil

Ingredients for garnishing

- 2–3 green chillies slit lengthwise
- A few sprigs of coriander, chopped

Method

- Heat oil in a cooker, add finely chopped onions and stir to ensure that the onions do not burn.
- When the onions turn light brown, add mutton, ginger-garlic paste, black elaichi, cloves, black pepper and cook for 3 minutes on a medium flame; stir well.
- Then add turmeric powder, red chilli powder, coriander powder and salt. Cook for a few minutes.
- Add chopped beetroot and tomatoes. Stir a little.
- Then add a little water and pressure cook the mutton and beetroot for 3 whistles.
- Once the mutton is cooked, leave on the flame till the water dries up. Keep sprinkling a little water and cook.

Add chopped coriander and sliced green chillies and stir for a little while till the oil separates.

◆   Switch off the gas and serve with chapattis or rice.

BENARASI ALOO

Ingredients

◆   500 gm cubed potatoes
◆   2 large onions, finely chopped
◆   3 tomatoes, chopped into medium cubes
◆   4 whole red chillies (preferably Madras red chillies)
◆   Oil to cook
◆   Salt to taste

Method

◆   Heat oil in a kadhai, add chopped onions and sauté.
◆   When the onions start turning light brown, add whole red chillies and fry until they are brown in colour and remove in a vessel.
◆   In the same kadhai, add cubed potatoes and fry for a minute or two.
◆   Then add the cut tomatoes.
◆   Sauté for a minute; add salt and a little water if necessary.
◆   When the tomato-potato mixture is half cooked, add the fried onions and chillies to it after crushing them. Cook till the potatoes are well done.
◆   Best enjoyed with rotis and steamed rice.

SAMBIT BAL, EDITOR-IN-CHIEF, ESPNCRICINFO

MOTHER: SASWATI BAL

I grew up in a small village, in a relatively remote part of Orissa that was untouched by city folks. My mother, Bou, had gone to spend the last few weeks of her pregnancy with my grandmother and was stranded there because my father's car broke down due to torrential rains. Such was the deluge that no one could step out for two days and so, I was born at home.

Bou tells me that, as if on cue, it stopped raining immediately after I was born, and even the car started working. A few months later, she conceived again, and since she was teaching in a school which was far away, she brought me back and entrusted me to the care of my grandparents. Looking back, I feel blessed, because throughout my life I had the love of two sets of parents.

I grew up with an intimacy with rural life that most children today can't even imagine. When I go back there now, I realize how idyllic the place was. My grandfather, the least worldly person I know, left the village to build a home on the outskirts, to be close to the mango orchard that he had inherited. The house was flanked by mountains on one side and all around us were fruit and berry trees—mango, jamun, guava, sitaphal. I spent my childhood climbing these trees, sleeping the odd night on machans they built on mango trees during the season. To sight a snake on the branches wasn't uncommon. The village pond, dotted with palm trees, was a couple of hundred metres away and the paddy fields not too far.

My grandparents were vegetarians, and I grew up that way just by observing them. And eating organic was not a conscious lifestyle choice: it was the way of life. Other than potatoes, onions and maybe some pulses, everything grew around us and vegetables were plucked only when they were to be cooked.

Growing up with my grandma, also Bou to me, my biggest indulgence was food; whatever she cooked was divine and a lot of my childhood was spent watching her in the kitchen. There were no gas stoves back then and everything was cooked on what we fancily describe today as a wood-fired chulha. There was no mixer-grinder and packaged powdered masalas were unheard of—all spices were ground fresh on stone or pestle and mortar, filling the house with delicious aromas.

We ate four meals daily. Breakfast would be a range of cereals—poha, kurmura, or chhatua (a mix of roasted and ground gram flours)—with milk or curd, bananas and grated coconut, or cooked stuff like upma or chakuli pitha (similar to dosa, but softer); lunch would be rice with dal or dalma (dal made with vegetable, and there is an array of dalmas with different dals and different tempering), something green or a sautéed seasonal vegetable and a curry; the 5 p.m. snack would be something savoury; and dinner would be a light affair with rotis and subzi.

One of my favourite childhood memories was sitting with Bou in the kitchen every morning, waiting for her to finish her other chores and put whatever was left of the milk to thicken over slow fire. It wasn't unlike rabdi, but a much thicker and darker version that stuck to the bottom of the utensil from which I would scrape the last morsel with my fingers before going to school.

The great thing about food those days was that everything was seasonal. You ate gobhi in winter, padwal in summer, and bhindi and papdi at the start of the rainy season. There was always a sense of anticipation, and you had to wait to eat your favourite veggies. Since everything grew in the backyard, you went and looked at the produce every day. Bou even grew our lentils in the backyard. I remember plucking the tuvar dal beans and eating them right off the pod. Rice was processed at home. Paddy would be boiled in huge containers and dried in the courtyards, and dehusked in the *dhinki*, the traditional husk lever made of hardwood. I now have a small farm off the Mumbai-Pune highway where I grow rice and some vegetables, and it's my way of reliving my beautiful childhood.

Bou cooked the same ingredients in a variety of ways, each distinctive and delicious. She used red pumpkin for several curries, and she batter-fried the pumpkin blossom into a delightful snack or, along with the stem, she made it into a flavourful curry. Raw bananas were fried, made into cutlets, used in many curries and dalmas, each tastier than the other.

Then there were the pithas, a broad and eclectic genre of festive food, which came in all sizes, shapes and texture. And Bou made them all—from memory, I can count at least twelve varieties. Pithas are made with a batter or dough of different combinations; they come in sweet and savoury varieties; some of them have fillings, mostly of a mixture of grated coconut, cottage cheese and jaggery; some are steamed, some are fried, some baked, and some are made on tawa; and each of this is a signature dish for a festival.

My favourite was poda (baked) pitha. It was made in two ways: sweet and savoury. I loved the savoury one, which was made with the same batter as idli, with chopped coconut and green chillies. My grandmother made it in a flattish earthen pot, which she layered with banana leaves before pouring the batter into it. She then covered the pitha with another layer of banana leaves and put coal on top. That way, it got cooked on both sides at the same time with a thick outer crust. You then cut it into cake-sized pieces, dipped it in home-made ghee and crushed green chillies and enjoyed it.

While we now try to replicate that in normal kadhais on a gas stove, flipping it over to cook on both sides, I look forward to my visits to Bhubaneswar where my mother, my other Bou, waits to make it for me.

The other thing that my grandma Bou made, and now my mother and sister-in-law never fail to make, was ghanta tarkari, a signature vegetarian dish with a medley of vegetables. The making of ghanta tarkari is almost an industrial effort that takes over two hours, most of it spent cutting the vegetables with precision.

In the decades since I left the village and moved to a megapolis, I have travelled around the world, and food has always been a big part of my travels. But nowhere have I come across a wider range, both in the ingredients used and style of cooking, than Orissa. We are known as fish-eating people, but the number of vegetables we eat and in the number of ways they are cooked, is quite astounding.

Apart from the usual tomato and onion, which came to the state much later, we have a whole range of mustard-based gravies, a range of khuskhus-based, milk-based and coconut-based gravies and stir-fries with minimal tempering. Some of the dishes are slightly sweet, some slightly tangy, some spicy and some tart. And then there are the roasted vegetables. Most of us are familiar with roasted baingan bharta, but Odias roast lots of other stuff too: bhindi, turai, tomatoes, which are then made into a bharta with chopped onions, green chillies, garlic and salt, a few drops of mustard oil and a pinch of water. Nothing can capture the original flavours than the smoky bits of vegetables floating in their own juices.

There is also pakhala, the simplest and the most basic of Odia staples. In villages, lots of people have it as their first meal before going off to the fields to work. The practice was to leave the leftover rice to ferment overnight with water and then add some chillies, salt and maybe a little curd in it. It can even be eaten with some onions on the side, but at home, it is an elaborate affair with an array of side dishes including fish fry, roasted vegetables, some greens and whatever else takes our fancy. Odia dreams are made of summer weekends with a sumptuous afternoon pakhala meal followed by a hearty snooze. Only to wake up to some bara and piyaji, our versions of medu vada and dal vada.

And no one makes them better than my mother. The Odia bara is one without the hole, but the crucial difference is the spicing of the batter. It has onions, ginger, green chillies, and when fried, the bara is less dense than the south Indian variety. The piyaji (the name comes from pyaaz or onion) is a lot fluffier. The secret, I think, is that my mother half fries them, lets them cool a bit, presses them in her palms so that the top cracks a bit and then fries them again, so they are crunchier and lighter.

I was a bit awkward around my parents when, at the age of eleven, I finally came to live with them. But one thing that came into my life properly then was non-vegetarian food. It took me a while to get used to the smell of fish, but mutton was easier to get used to. It was the Sunday fix. During college years, it became my job to buy mutton on Sunday mornings, a responsibility I took quite seriously. And even when I had household help, Bou would always make the mutton curry herself. The homestyle Odia mutton curry is thinner, always cooked with potatoes and eaten at lunch with rice, but it was a time-consuming process, because perfect mutton curry needs slow-cooking.

It was not until I came to live in Mumbai by myself that I learnt to cook, but one of my fondest memories in the kitchen was helping Bou make chapattis in our Bhubaneswar home. She would roll the chapattis, sitting on the floor, and I would roast them on the tawa, and every chapatti that fluffed into the perfect orb felt like a triumph. But more than that, it was the unspoken bonding that it created with Bou that I cherish the most.

ENDURI PITHA

Ingredients

- 1 1/2 cup rice
- 1 cup urad dal
- 1 cup grated coconut
- 100 gm freshly made paneer
- 150 gm jaggery, the sticky variety is preferable
- 3 small cardamoms
- 6 peppercorns
- Salt to taste
- Green turmeric leaves

Method

◆ Soak rice and urad dal together for about 4 hours and
   grind them coarsely.
◆ Add salt, whip the batter well and leave it to ferment
   overnight.
◆ For the stuffing, mix the grated coconut, jaggery and
   paneer with your hand. (At home, paneer is always made
   fresh: split one litre of milk with four spoons of vinegar
   mixed with a little water.)
◆ Put the mixture in a frying pan on medium flame for a
   few minutes, stirring it constantly so that it doesn't burn.
   When it's dry, add powdered cardamom and black pepper.
   Mix well and keep aside.
◆ Now, take one whole green turmeric leaf (if it is very long;
   you may want to cut it into half to get two parts; it's easier
   to manage), open it wide and flat on a thali and spread the
   batter thinly across the whole leaf.
◆ Then scoop the stuffing with a spoon and heap it lengthwise
   in the middle. You have to decide on the amount of stuffing
   based on the size of the leaf and bearing in mind that you
   have to fold the leaf and seal it like a sandwich.
◆ My grandmother always used an earthen pot, but you can
   use any wide-mouthed pot that has a ledge protruding
   outwards to facilitate the tying of the cloth around (even
   the base of a five-litre pressure cooker will do), half fill it
   with water, and tie a thin but firm cloth (muslin preferably)
   on the top.
◆ Place the folded pitha carefully on top, cover it with a
   concave lid and steam it till done. You can use the steamer
   baskets used to make momos, I guess, though I have never
   tried it.

* Remove, and let it cool a bit before unwrapping and digging in.
* Handy tip: Leave it wrapped till you are ready to eat.
* And, can you make it without the turmeric leaves? You could get the texture right with banana leaves perhaps, but never the flavour. That's why it's a seasonal dish. It is made on the occasion of Prathamastami, a festival that is celebrated for the eldest child of the generation, between November and December.

* * *

GHANTA TARKARI

Ingredients

* 500 gm white pumpkin
* Potatoes
* Colocasia roots (sarru)
* Yam potatoes (desi alu)
* Ridge gourd (janhi)
* String beans (bara gudi)
* Broad beans (shima or papdi, as they are called in Marathi)
* Brinjal (baingan)
* Radish
* Elephant apple (oou; should be half cooked and added to the vegetables in the pot only towards the end)
* Red pumpkin
* 1 coconut, half grated, the other half sliced in small pieces
* Sprouts (of red chana or buta-black or red chickpeas, half cooked and whole moong)
* 1 tbs oil of choice

- 1 tsp of turmeric powder
- 1 tsp 5 spices (paanch phoron)
- 3–4 dry red chillies
- 2-inch piece of grated ginger
- 1 tsp roasted cumin powder
- 1/2 tsp cumin seeds
- 1 tsp red chilli powder
- 1 tbs ghee
- Salt to taste
- 1 small piece of jaggery to taste
- (The rest of the vegetables together should be less than half a kg. Most importantly, the red pumpkin must be well ripened)

Method

- In a wok, take about 1 tbs of oil, add the vegetables, turmeric and salt. Stir and cover.
- Meanwhile, in a bit of ghee, sauté cubed coconut, grated coconut and sprouts.
- Add the above mix to the vegetables.
- Once the vegetables are tender, turn off the gas.
- Take a fresh wok, add equal amounts of ghee and oil, and wait for the oil to heat up.
- Now add: 5 spices (paanch phoron), dry red chillies, grated ginger, jeera and a small piece of jaggery.
- Now pour the vegetables into the seasoning and let it simmer for 5–7 minutes.
- Garnish with roasted cumin and red chilli powder mix.
- The above-mentioned powder is almost a staple spice in Odia households. In order to add the true flavour and authenticity, this is made instantly when required, by dry

roasting 2–3 dry red chillies and a tablespoon of whole cumin and then making a powder using the grinding stone or pestle. For enhanced flavour, I throw in a few fenugreek (methi) seeds for roasting.

KAKHARU PHOOLA BHAJA

Ingredients

- 10 pumpkin flowers
- 1/2 cup rice/rice flour
- 1 tbs besan
- 1 tsp cumin seeds
- 2–3 dry red chillies
- 4 garlic cloves
- 1-inch ginger
- 1/4 tsp turmeric powder
- Refined cooking oil
- Salt to taste

Method

- If you want to make it the authentic way, make the batter from scratch. Soak the rice in water for about an hour and then grind it in the mixer with cumin seeds, garlic and ginger, and leave it slightly coarse. Alternatively, you can make the batter by adding water to rice flour and besan. Add turmeric powder, chilli powder, salt and mix well.
- Prepare the flower by chopping the stem at the bottom and removing the inner parts. But make sure you have the whole flower. Wash it under water running and allow the water to drain off.

- Heat a pan on medium flame and slather it with a generous amount of oil.
- Dip the flowers one by one in the batter, and put them on the pan. After they have turned crisp on one side, flip them and fry till both the sides turn golden brown.
- In Odia households, it's an accompaniment with lunch, but I have discovered it can be a wonderful snack with drinks or otherwise.

SANDIP SOPARRKAR, DANCER, CHOREOGRAPHER AND ACTOR

MOTHER: RANI SOPARRKAR

I have this amazing childhood memory of Mom in the kitchen on Sunday mornings when she would make our special weekend breakfast: kheer-poori. She would sing while cooking it: '*Kheer-poori khayenge, Dilli ki dulhan layenge,*' and my brother and I would be in splits. Decades later, when I got married, my wife did turn out to be from Delhi!

Mom would say kheer is like dance: the milk and rice are the personality of the dancer—her looks, posture, carriage, etc. She likened the cooking of the kheer to the dedication and commitment of a dancer because it takes patience to get both right. The costumes and jewellery are as important to the dancer as almonds and raisins are for garnishing the kheer, she would say; and, finally, the sugar in the kheer is like the dancer's technique—it has to be just right—too much technique and it will take away the charm of the performance just like too much sugar spoils the kheer! I can never eat a plate of kheer-poori without remembering Mom singing in the kitchen about our Dilli ki dulhan.

I grew up in a family of four—my brother, parents and I—and because Dad worked in the army, we travelled the length and breadth of the country, going wherever his posting took us.

I remember, in those days, Mom would constantly cook for her two boys who were growing up faster than she could keep pace. We had huge appetites and would eat over a dozen parathas each and she would look at us in exasperation and say, '*Thak gayi hoon parathe bana bana ke. Band karo ab* [I'm tired from making parathas endlessly, stop eating now]!'

In those days, when we ate parathas four times a day, I think she would have collapsed if she had to make anything else such as dosas for the three men in her life.

She would make plain ones for breakfast because she too had to go to work after sending us to school. Her repertoire of parathas included methi, mooli and what she called the navlakha paratha. For the longest time we were dazzled by the name, imagining we were eating something grand, till we realized it was actually made from leftover vegetables and dal mixed together. But it did taste delicious, and I remember tucking into quite a few of those with great gusto.

It has been a couple of decades since I left my parents' home in Pune but when I visit them, I still nag Mom to make sabudana khichdi for me. My grandparents stayed with us for a few years when we were kids, and since Grandma would eat only sabudana khichdi on her fasting days, Mom learnt the recipe from her. Of course, the entire family soon got hooked to it, and my brother and I started eating it along with our regular parathas on Grandma's fasting days. Some of those food memories remain in our mind and on our palate forever and that is the reason why I am a fan of kheer-poori and sabudana khichdi.

Mom's cooking was influenced by every part of the country we lived in. In Srinagar or Jammu, we ate Kashmiri-style mutton with parathas. The domestic help at every posting was from the local community, and Mom would inevitably learn some dishes from them. When we were in Jaipur, Mom made local dishes like panjiri, dal bhaati and other goodies. When we were in college, the food varied—some days it would be rajma chawal and some days sambar chawal. When we were in Bhopal, the non-vegetarian dishes were mostly chicken, while in J&K, it was largely mutton. The pleasant fallout from all the diversity is that today I eat whatever is served at the table without fussing.

In Assam, we lived in a bungalow on a hilltop with a jackfruit tree next to the house. Mom decided she should make full use of the produce of the land, and so, every day we had dishes made from jackfruit—katal ki subzi, achar, halwa—till we had katal coming out of our ears! Mom was very clear that there was no question of wasting food. In our home in Pune, Mom told the gardener to plant some greens in our sprawling kitchen garden and he planted palak all over. For an entire month, there was a palak festival on our dining table. We protested like crazy then, but now I appreciate what we learnt through that experience. I know now that each vegetable can be made in a dozen different ways, to keep boredom at bay.

Mom made delicious gujiyas on festivals such as Holi, making some 200 of them at a time because my brother and I ate them at every hour of the day, wandering around the house. In the end, she got so tired of the gluttony that she laid down rules for us—she would make the goodies only once, and we could either eat them all in a day or over the week. The gujiyas would be kept in a huge box, and Mom probably hoped that they would last at least for the duration of the festival. We thought she was lazy back then, because other moms made sweets through the festive season. Now we know that she was not just tired but also worried about our weight—both my brother and I were obese and needed to eat less.

When I look back, I am horrified by how much we ate in those days. Dad fell ill when we were in college, and that's when we realized the importance of healthy eating.

Mom started making a variety of soupy stews for us with chicken or mutton to have at dinner and parathas became only a breakfast or lunch fare, minus the ghee. Kheer became a monthly affair instead of our weekly treats and that too with minimal sugar. She stopped making gujiyas after Dad took ill and today if we crave it, we buy a few pieces from a store and eat them.

Maybe it was all that cooking she did for us when we were growing up, but Mom now harbours a healthy aversion to the kitchen. If I request her to cook one of my childhood favourites, she laughs, saying she is done with that part of her life and is happy to eat whatever comes to the table, cooked by our domestic help.

Her cooking influenced my choice of career and she was thrilled when I decided to take up hospitality management. I studied at the Food Craft Institute and that was the only time Mom got a bit of relief from the endless cooking. I was so interested in my craft that I would come home and practise the dishes that were taught in class because the girls in my group never allowed me to cook and relegated me to washing dishes. I was so overenthusiastic about cooking that we would have enough to even feed the neighbours.

Mom made sure we helped around the house. She shopped for fresh groceries herself, and today I do the same despite having domestic help. She trained my brother and me to

INGaria

make chai for her and Dad, lay the table, chop veggies and help around the house. That made me independent and also developed my interest in the kitchen. Old habits die hard. Every morning, even now, I need to have two parathas for breakfast; without them, I feel something is missing in the day.

RICE KHEER

Ingredients

- 1/4 cup rice, basmati rice is best
- 1 tsp ghee
- 3–4 green cardamom pods, slightly crushed
- 1 litre whole milk
- 50–60 gm sugar (adjust to taste)
- 3 tbs chopped nuts (cashews, almonds, pistachios and raisins)
- A pinch of saffron

Method

- Rinse the rice and soak for 20–30 minutes. Drain and set aside.
- Heat a heavy-bottomed pan on medium flame. Add 1 tsp of ghee and add the soaked and drained rice. Also add 3–4 crushed green cardamom pods.
- Toss the rice with the ghee and cardamom for a couple of minutes, stirring constantly until it turns aromatic.
- Then add the milk to the pan and stir well. Set the heat to medium–high.
- Let the milk come to a boil; this will take around 10–12 minutes. Stir in between so that the milk doesn't stick to the bottom of the pan.

- Once the milk has come to a boil, lower the flame and let the kheer simmer for around 25 minutes.
- Stir every 2 minutes or so. After 25 minutes, the rice will soften and the kheer thicken. If you want it very thick, cook for 15 more minutes at this point.
- Add in the sugar and mix. Also add in the nuts.
- Cook the kheer for 5 more minutes. The sugar should dissolve completely. Don't worry if your kheer doesn't look very thick at this point. It will continue to thicken as it cools down.
- Remove the pan from the heat. Stir in saffron. Garnish with more nuts and serve the kheer warm or chilled.

GUJIYA

Ingredients for the filling

- 200 gm khoya
- 1 tbs powdered green cardamom
- 1/4 cup semolina
- 1 cup sugar
- 2–3 tsp finely chopped and roasted dry fruits (almonds, cashews, pistachios and raisins)

For the dough

- 4 cups all-purpose flour
- 1 1/2 cup ghee
- 1/4 cup water

Method

- Mix together all-purpose flour and water along with some ghee to knead it into a soft dough and keep aside for 60 minutes.
- In a deep frying pan, roast khoya and semolina till they turn golden and keep them aside to cool.
- To prepare the filling, add sugar, green cardamom and dry fruits to the cooled khoya and mix well.
- Roll out pooris from the dough and fill them with the stuffing along one side and fold the other side over, sealing the edges in such a way that it secures the stuffing while frying. Roll the sides as per your choice of pattern.
- Heat ghee in a pan over medium flame. Fry the gujiyas till golden brown on all sides, garnish them with some saffron strands and crushed pistachios.

CHICKEN STEW

Ingredients

- 1 kg boneless, skinless chicken breasts
- 2 tbs butter
- 2 large carrots, peeled and sliced round
- 1 stalk celery, chopped
- Salt and freshly ground black pepper to taste
- 1 tbs all-purpose flour
- 3 sprigs fresh thyme
- 1 bay leaf
- 300 gm baby potatoes, quartered
- 3 cups low-sodium chicken broth
- Freshly chopped parsley, for garnishing

Method

- Melt butter in a large pot over medium heat, add carrots and celery and season with salt and pepper.
- Cook, stirring often, until vegetables are tender (about 5 minutes).
- Add flour and stir until the vegetables are coated, then add chicken, thyme, bay leaf, potatoes and the broth. Season with salt and pepper.
- Bring the mixture to a simmer and cook until the chicken is no longer pink and potatoes are tender, for about 15 minutes.
- Remove from heat and transfer chicken to a medium bowl.
- Using two forks, shred the chicken into small pieces and garnish with parsley before serving.

SATYEN V. KOTHARI, FOUNDER AND CHIEF EXECUTIVE OFFICER, CUBE, SERIAL ENTREPRENEUR

MOTHER: NEENA KOTHARI

As a little boy of ten or twelve years of age with a huge appetite, one of my favourite meals cooked by my Ma was a simple dish of spicy masoor dal with fresh pavs, hot off the oven. The four of us would sit around the dining table in our small apartment in suburban Mumbai and dip the buttery pavs into the dal to soak it all up. It was an anytime meal for us and the spicy dal with onions, tomatoes and garlic was usually leftover from dinner, but was tastier the next morning. It was such a favourite that I would eat eight to nine pavs within minutes!

When my daughter and I were at home during the pandemic-induced lockdown recently, I remember calling Ma up and requesting her to instruct my domestic help to prepare the same dal for us.

When I left home to study at Stanford, I took the masoor dal recipe with me, never imagining that this simple dish would make me a star among my classmates. Every Thursday, a couple of friends—a German and an American—and I would take turns to cook the meal. It was the era of *Friends* and *Seinfeld* and we would watch telly and pig out the dishes we prepared. I made a variety of vegetarian meals, but the masoor dal was a big hit, with frequent repeat orders from friends who tasted it. It is Ma's classic that has followed me into my forties.

The other specialty by Ma that stands out in my memory is her fried garlic in ghee—whole pieces of garlic fried in home-made ghee and salt was one of the things she would cook for my brother and me when I was about four years old. It was a heavenly treat during the bitter winters of Pune and my brother and I would often fight over the last piece. Even today, when I miss the good old days or have a sore throat, I make myself this magic dish. When my daughter was recovering from a horrible accident in Italy a few months ago, one of the first things she asked for was fried garlic. That was how she got her mojo back.

The other Kothari family special is chokha ni dashmi (rice flour bhakri). This was our weekend treat for late breakfast, and I remember Ma would bring it fresh off the tawa while we sat at the table, savouring the soft bhakris with spicy pickles.

Then there was another dashmi meal we looked forward to—dashmi, bateta nu shaak (subzi) and a katori of milk. The extended Kothari family loved it too. We would take a chunk of dashmi, scoop up some shaak, dip the entire thing into the milk and eat it. I loved drinking the milk left in the bowl, which, by the end of the meal, would turn colourful from the turmeric and red chillies from the shaak.

Ma's standout dessert was dudhi ka halwa. I hate dudhi in any other form, but her halwa was and continues to be irresistible. When I was a teenager, Ma bought some sort of

Inframatic gadget, putting money together, bit by bit, to get the treasured possession home. She started making the most amazing stuffed omelettes, sandwiches and snacks in it. We were on a sticky wicket financially back then, but I remember her generously treating visiting cousins and guests to goodies made in the gadget. The guests got to eat first and if there was something left, she divided it between my brother and me. Years later, when I got back from Stanford, I still remembered the sandwiches made in the gadget and asked Ma if we could buy one of those for the house, but sadly, it was no longer available in the market.

On some weekend mornings, my brother and I would set the table and make breakfast for our parents—eggs and freshly squeezed orange juice. My parents beamed with happiness, and I feel grateful today that we could do it for them. Our family had fairly Westernized preferences for that time—home-made pizzas and sandwiches that Ma made for us. There was not a lot of disposable income for Ma to buy stuff from outside, so the pizza was mostly just tomato sauce, chopped capsicum and lots of cheese put on a bhakri (Indian flat bread made from jowar or rice flour) and baked on top of a tawa. I remember I once ate eight of those pizzas out of sheer greed and was so sick the next day that I went off pizza for months.

Diwali was a joyous celebration with the extended family. We visited relatives and food headlined every visit, but I had eyes only for the shiny rows of glasses in the fridge, brimming with orange-coloured squash.

Dal, bhat, shak and rotli was our family staple, but because Dad felt the boys in our extended family were short and weak, he introduced us to non-vegetarian food. The drill was that we had to eat chicken and meat and a minimum of four rotis.

Maybe he was right, because my brother and I are now the tallest men in our family. But at fourteen, I started rebelling, insisting I would no longer eat dal-bhat, so my parents started introducing other interesting food into our meals.

Just before I went abroad to study, Ma gave me a few lessons on cooking basic food—how to make a dosa, masoor dal, her biryani, different preparations with potatoes and even the processes to follow when cooking a good meal. For instance, when to add onions in a dish, at what point to add the masala, etc. I am so grateful she did that. It's because of her that my brother and I didn't become the stereotypical Indian men who are clueless in the kitchen.

Life has come a full circle for our family. Just before my daughter, Zoe, went to Italy last year for her studies, I found myself teaching her to make basic dishes so she could eat the food that she likes and it included the masoor dal! It would fill me with joy when my phone would ring and it would be her, sending me pictures of one of the dishes she had cooked.

AKKHA MASOOR NI DAL

Ingredients

- 2 cups whole masoor
- 1/2 tsp turmeric powder
- 1 tbs coriander-cumin powder
- 1 tsp garam masala
- 1/2 tsp cumin seeds
- A pinch of asafoetida
- 1 large onion, chopped finely
- 2 large tomatoes, chopped finely

- 1/2 tsp each ginger and garlic paste
- Oil for seasoning

Method

- Soak the masoor for at least an hour.
- Take 2 tsp of oil and temper it with cumin and asafoetida; sauté onions till golden brown.
- Add garlic ginger paste and sauté for another 2 minutes.
- Add salt to taste, turmeric, coriander-cumin powder and garam masala. Sauté again for 2 minutes.
- Add 2 large chopped tomatoes and let them cook until soft. Keep stirring in between.
- Now add soaked masoor and 4 cups of water and bring it to boil.
- Then let it simmer for 30–40 minutes or until the masoor is cooked and is a bit thickish in consistency.
- Garnish it with fresh coriander and a squeeze of lemon. This is great with buttered pav, bread slices or even steamed rice and rotis.

DUDHI HALWA

Ingredients

- 1 medium-sized bottle gourd (approximately 300 gm, grated)
- 2 cups full fat milk
- 3 tbs ghee (home-made ghee is best)
- 1 1/2 cups sugar or as preferred
- 3 tsp sliced almonds
- 3 tsp rose petals (optional)
- 1/2 tsp powdered cardamom powder

Method

* Take the bottle gourd and grate it on a medium-sized grater.
* In a heavy-bottomed pan, heat the ghee and sauté the grated dudhi till it starts to change colour.
* Now add milk and let it cook on a medium flame, stirring it occasionally.
* Make sure the dudhi does not burn or stick to the bottom of the pan.
* Once the milk has evaporated and the mixture has turned thick, add the sugar and cook it till the mixture becomes thicker.
* Stir it continuously. Once done, add the cardamom powder and spread it on a plate. Garnish with sliced almonds and rose petals.
* Can be enjoyed both chilled or sizzling hot.

SHANTA GOKHALE, AUTHOR

MOTHER: INDIRA GHOKHALE

Aai has been gone for a long time but sometimes, when I am cooking or supervising the cooking for a special occasion, my mind goes back to her. She was a versatile, talented and passionate cook, and left her distinct mark on everything she cooked.

When she got married and moved to her marital home, she knew mostly Konkanastha Brahmin recipes that she had inherited from her mother and grandmother, but she soon discovered that her husband was very fond of meat and fish. The young bride, a pure vegetarian herself, took on the challenge and gradually learnt to cook delicious meat recipes from the wife of a Kolhapuri friend of her husband. Another of his friends taught her traditional fish recipes from coastal Sawantwadi. Aai's happiest times were in the kitchen, pampering us with the endless dishes she seemed to conjure up so that mealtimes at home were never boring.

Aai was also a quick learner and very experimental when it came to cooking. Growing up in Mumbai's Shivaji Park, it was normal for us to walk over to the beach along with the neighbourhood kids and eat bhelpuri from the vendors who hawked their stuff there. She could not bear the thought that her children were eating bhelpuri made by a stranger, so she decided to learn to prepare it at home. We were fascinated by her determination as she made multiple trips to the bhelpuri-wallah, tasting the bhel and experimenting at home, till she figured out exactly what went into the making of the snack. When she finally perfected the dish, everything that went into it, including the kadak puris and sev, were made at home. Only the murmura was outsourced, and I remember how we kids ate it greedily, with no complaints because it was even better than what we ate at the beach.

I inherited the recipes from her, and it is now a family ritual for us to have a weekly or fortnightly bhel evening when I prepare it for my son and daughter-in-law who love the snack. Reminds me of the good old days.

Ours was a family that was held together by food in many ways. My father was a great believer in the goodness of balanced diets. His love for nutritional meals ensured that our plates always had the staples that make a balanced Maharashtrian thaali—aamti, bhaji, poli and koshimbir. For some reason, he was anti-rice and so it appeared on our plates only in the form of masala bhaat, sakhari bhaat or narali bhaat.

We were a family of atheists and didn't have any idols of Gods in our house, but we celebrated every festival, food being at the centre of it all. Be it Ganesh Chaturthi or Diwali, there was a social rather than religious element to the festivities at home that called for a great deal of food being cooked. I like to think of our festivals as food festivals and so, Diwali was about a toran at the door, firecrackers and lots of faral (snacks and sweets). I remember, in those days, Shivaji Park was a new locality that was being developed, and in our lane everyone knew one another—Gujaratis, Chandraseniya

Kayastha Prabhus, Saraswats, East Indians, Malayalis. All of us celebrated festivals by exchanging sweets prepared in our homes, and it was wonderful community living.

Aai would make huge quantities of faral and we would walk up and down the road delivering platefuls of shev, chakli, shankarpale, besan ladoo and chirote to the families in our tight-knit community. Aai made the most delicate-looking and tasty chirote. One of my special pre-teen Diwali memories is of helping her make them. It was a truly magical experience. Seven roundels of white-and-pink-tinted dough were rolled out thin and stacked with a smearing of a ghee-and-corn-flour paste in between, rolled into a log and cut into discs which were flattened and rolled out lightly. When these puris went into the hot ghee, the layers unfurled and soon we had a pile of pink-and-white 'roses', ready to be sprinkled with powdered sugar. My eldest kaka (paternal uncle) loved this delicacy, and every Diwali, a tin packed with chirote was dispatched to him in Nashik. When I set up my own home, I tried making chirote, but failed. Discouraged, I never tried again. But the other day, a school friend told me she makes them every Diwali the way Aai taught her. It warmed my heart to know that someone was carrying her legacy forward.

For Diwali, Aai also prepared very special karanjis that we all looked forward to. These were made by rolling out multiple chapattis, layering them with a whipped-up cream of ghee and corn flour, gathering them into a tight roll, cutting the roll into one-inch pieces, putting a spoonful of coconut stuffing in them, folding them in crescents, cutting the extra pastry with a karanji cutter and frying them in ghee on a medium flame. This made all the layers bloom. She often added edible colour to alternate chapattis to emphasize the layers so that they emerged from the kadhai bursting with colour and flavour.

The arrival of Lord Ganpati was much looked forward to in our home—even though we never had an idol installed—because Aai made delicious modaks. Her modaks were so delicate and good looking that we did not have the heart to bite into them. The family ate the modaks with dollops of ghee. I have followed that tradition, and even today my kids look forward to me preparing modaks for them during Ganapati.

One of my favourites from Aai's faral repertoire was her chakli. In fact, I was so besotted with chaklis that they were a staple in my *dabba* (school tiffin box). In school, I used to be called 'chakli', because every single day the chakli would make an appearance in my tiffin box to the endless amusement of my friends.

Unlike today, when everybody has the luxury of going on YouTube and getting recipes off the Internet, my sister and I learnt the finer nuances of cooking by helping Aai in the kitchen and watching her cook. The bonus, of course, was getting to eat even as the food was being cooked. I would help her make papad in summers, and the carrot there for me was getting to eat the spicy dangar—the dough with which the papad is made—dipped in oil. I still salivate when I remember how it felt on my tongue.

Aai's ghadichya polya—soft, delicate, layered chapattis—were a treat. On some evenings, I would stand beside her as she rolled the polis and devour them as they came hot off the tawa, without any accompaniment. It remains my comfort food all these decades later.

I loved everything she prepared but the usals she made—matki, masoor and fresh matar (green peas)—were my favourites. And her delicious aamti is part of my repertoire even today; it's the best comfort food for the days when we all need comforting. After I got married, I got her to give me a few recipes, which proved very handy when my husband and I settled abroad for some time. She was happy that I cooked every day even when I was in England and loved that I would call her up for more recipes.

At *Femina*, where I worked for several years, I was in charge of the food and fiction sections, and even if it was nepotism in some ways, I once asked the then editor, Vimla Patil, if I could feature some of Aai's recipes in the magazine. She agreed, and Aai was thrilled to bits that her talent and recipes got publicity in such an esteemed magazine. Among others, her specialities—pudachi karanje and chirote—were featured in the magazine.

Aai was also an extraordinary experimenter in the kitchen, often mixing and matching ingredients or dramatically changing recipes to come up with her own version of a traditional dish. Vaatli dal, served in Maharashtrian homes, was one such recipe that she reinvented. While the original dish—coarsely ground chickpeas seasoned with cumin, mustard seeds, hing and curry leaves—is usually dry in texture, Aai came up with a new version that became an instant winner. Always on the lookout for interesting snacks to serve the ladies who came home to attend her bhajan classes, she came up with a smashing version of the vaatli dal to which she added soaked sabudana, finely chopped onions, coconut and fresh coriander leaves. The soaked sabudana lent moisture and softened the ground chickpeas, making the dish a conversation piece among the bhajan *mandali* (group).

For years, Aai and I discussed publishing a book of her recipes—the decades of experimental cooking needed documentation, I would tell her, and she would laugh and be excited about the prospect. Sadly, it was never to be because she was diagnosed with cancer and took the news badly. She could never understand how she, with all the attention she paid to nutrition and healthy eating, could be stricken with the disease. After her cancer surgery, she spent ten days with me, so I could take care of her, and I hoped we could use that precious time to get those recipes down. But a point comes when you give up on life, and in the days after the surgery, Aai gave up on her life. I never managed to take down the recipes and they went away with her. She passed away in 1986 at the age of seventy-three. But each time I make one of her recipes, I am reminded of her. It is like she is with me when I am cooking that dish.

DAALIMBYAANCH BIRDA

Ingredients

- 1 cup field beans
- 1 small onion, chopped
- 2 tbs grated coconut
- 3 peppercorns
- 1 tsp coriander seeds
- 1/2 tsp cumin seeds
- 2 cloves
- 1/4 inch piece cinnamon
- 1 tsp mustard seeds
- 1/4 tsp asafoetida
- 1/2 tsp turmeric
- 4 green chillies
- Salt and chilli powder as per taste
- A small lemon-sized ball of tamarind, soaked and juice extracted
- Jaggery as per taste

Method

• Soak the beans for two days in warm water, drain, tie up in a muslin cloth to allow them to sprout. Remove sprouted beans into a bowl of very warm water. This loosens the skin.

• Then follows the rather tedious process of popping the beans out of their skins. In my mother's days, this was done by spreading them on a *paat* (the flat wooden seat on which one sat for meals) and pressing them down with your thumbs, so you did two beans at a time. I would often help my mother at this task. These days, in Mumbai, you get ready sprouted beans. Somebody else has done the job for you, at a price!

• Pressure cook the beans in water. The number of whistles depends on how long the beans take to cook.

• Dry roast and grind to a paste 1 small onion, 2 tbs grated coconut, 3 peppercorns, 1 tsp coriander seeds, 1/2 tsp cumin seeds, 2 cloves, small piece cinnamon.

• Heat 2 tbs oil, and add 1 flat tsp mustard seeds. When they start to splutter, add 1/2 tsp cumin seeds, 1/4 tsp asafoetida, 1/2 tsp turmeric and chopped onion. Fry till the onion is soft.

• Add 3–4 pieces of green chillies and the coconut masala and fry for a couple of minutes.

• Add the cooked beans along with the cooking water, salt and chilli powder to taste.

• End with tamarind pulp and jaggery and let the whole thing simmer for 5 minutes.

• This is a gravy dish and supposed to be hot enough to make your eyes water and your nose run.

SABUDAANYAACHE VADE

Ingredients

* 1 cup sabudana, washed
* 2 medium-sized potatoes
* 1 or 2 green chillies
* Half a cup of peanuts
* 1 tsp cumin seeds
* Salt to taste
* Oil for frying

Method

* Wash 1 cup sabudana 2 or 3 times till the water runs almost clear. Drain, cover and keep for 2 hours.
* Boil and mash 2 medium potatoes.
* Cut 1 green chilli into small pieces.
* Roast, skin and coarsely pound half a cup of peanuts.
* Mix all these ingredients together along with salt to taste and 1 tsp of cumin seeds. Knead lightly.
* Make equal-sized balls. Flatten them between your palms and shallow fry in a mixture of ghee and oil. (My mother used only ghee but times have changed.)
* The oil/ghee should be fairly hot because the sabudana needs to puff up; but not so hot that the vade burn before the sabudana cooks.
* Remove on to kitchen paper.
* The vade have to be eaten hot otherwise they lose their crispness.

- We serve them with thick, home-made dahi. The uninitiated eat them with tomato ketchup.

BOTTLE GOURD WITH CASHEW NUTS
(MY MOTHER'S INVENTION)

Ingredients

- 4 cups cubed bottle gourd
- 1 cup cashew nut halves
- 1 cup milk
- 1 tbs ghee
- 3/4 tsp cumin seeds
- 1/4 tsp asafoetida
- 2 green chillies cut into largish pieces
- 1/2 cup grated coconut
- 1 tsp sugar
- Salt to taste
- Coriander leaves for garnishing

Method

- Heat ghee and add cumin seeds.
- When they start to splutter and change colour, add hing and chilli pieces.
- When their aroma rises, put in the cubed gourd and cashew nut pieces.
- Add a little water, cover and allow to half cook.
- Then add milk, salt and sugar and cook fully.
- Garnish with grated coconut and finely chopped coriander leaves.

DESERT DELIGHT (RECIPE AND THE NAME ARE BOTH MY MOTHER'S INVENTIONS)

Ingredients

* 1 cup soft, black seedless dates
* 1/2 cup sugar
* 1/4 cup coarsely chopped walnuts
* 1/4 cup grated and lightly roasted dry coconut
* A little ghee

Method

* Mash the dates. Mix well with sugar and cook to a sticky consistency. If you drop a little bit in cold water, you should be able to roll it into a ball which makes a clean clicking sound against a plate.
* Add walnuts to this mixture.
* Drizzle ghee round the edges and lift the lump out on to a flat, greased surface, cover with a sheet of polythene and roll out to a rectangle of 1/4 inch thickness.
* Sprinkle the roasted coconut on it evenly.
* Roll tight and cut into half inch roundels.

GUL POLI

Ingredients for gul

* 7 cups grated jaggery
* 1 1/2 cups grated dry coconut
* 3/4 cup sesame seeds

- 1 tbs besan
- 1 tbs oil

Method

- Dry roast coconut and sesame seeds and grind them together. Lightly roast besan.
- Put jaggery into a heavy-bottomed pan on medium heat. As soon as it melts and there are no lumps left, take it off the stove and add the other ingredients.
- Stir to mix well.
- Cover and set aside to cool.
- Then knead it into a smooth ball.

Ingredients for poli

- 7 cups atta (wheat flour)
- 7 tbs oil

Method

- Mix the atta with water and knead together. The consistency has to be exactly the same as the consistency of the gul stuffing. This allows the gul to spread evenly on the poli.
- Now roll 2 puris of the dough and pat one puri of the gul. The stuffing should be equal in size to the dough taken for one of the puris.
- Place the pat of stuffing on one puri. Lay the second puri on top. Pinch edges to seal the stuffing in.
- Roll thin with an even movement, using rice flour to stop the poli from sticking.

- Roast the poli on a tawa over medium heat, turning over when one side gets light-brown spots.
- The secret is to get the consistency of the dough and stuffing and the temperature of the tawa right. Then making gul polis is a breeze. Otherwise, it's a mess with gul leaking out and spoiling the tawa. If this happens, keep kitchen paper and oil handy. You will have to clean the tawa with oil before you roast the next poli. Gul polis must be eaten with dollops of home-made ghee.

SHASHI THAROOR, MP, AUTHOR

MOTHER: LILY THAROOR

I will always associate Mummy's cooking with traditional Kerala food—a variety of malakushyams, upperis, mezhukkuvarattis and other dishes that I relished as a child and adore even today.

Mummy, Lily Tharoor, married right out of high school and went off to London with my father. By twenty, she was already a busy mother. When my parents returned to India, my father's job required them to move cities frequently, because of which Mummy could not maintain a stable career.

Mummy wanted her kids to see her as a woman with many creative pursuits. She had a great creative energy that she spent on doing innumerable things. During my high school days, when we lived in Kolkata, she learnt Rabindra Sangeet, singing it in a beautiful voice though occasionally lapsing into her Malayali accent. She also learnt Thanjavur painting and one of her works, a Ganesha on glass, adorns my living room.

While in Kolkata, she embarked on a pickle-making venture, pursuing her new-found passion diligently and experimenting extensively to develop the product range. 'Lily's Pickles' eventually featured eleven pickle varieties, for which she would frequently visit the neighbourhood bottling and canning factory to supervise production. Later, she published her own *Book of Pickles* with recipes for family and friends. Few probably know that in the 1960s and 1970s she wrote a column, 'Household Hints', first for *Eve's Weekly* and then for *Femina*. These columns too were put together for a privately-published book, copies of which are now with our extended family in various parts of the world.

Back in school, I was a scrawny kid who could eat a lot and still be thin and wiry. While I got my favourite vegetarian food, Mummy ensured that chicken and mutton dishes were prepared for my sisters, Shobha and Smita. Mummy didn't really want to be recognized as a cook, she just made sure that food was properly prepared for us. But the Kerala dishes were her domain and her knowledge and hands influenced them.

I remember her delicious spinach malakushyam, a dish that was perfect with steaming hot rice. Her urulakizhangu upperi set the taste buds and our mouths on fire, but I could never have enough of it. Although Mummy and I disliked brinjal, she would occasionally toss a few brinjals into the sambar for my father—mother and son would, of course, skip it!

I left home at the age of sixteen to go to Delhi for my studies, but would frequently feel the pull of Mummy's pachadis, parippus, thorans, upperis and a few north Indian dishes she cooked occasionally.

Mummy believed that children had to eat well to grow well and so, throughout our childhood, we were served a fairly heavy high tea around 4.30 p.m.—there would be bondas, pakodas, bhajjis and dosas. To this day, I am fond of eating dosas in the evening, though I have retained the habit of having idlis for breakfast. Mummy also served us dessert after every lunch and dinner. She made excellent payasam, but I preferred

Western desserts. I still remember her pineapple upside down cake and sherry trifle, both lingering influences from her London days; and we both are chocoholics, perhaps because she munched on chocolates when she was expecting me!

Birthdays were special in many ways. It was a family tradition that the birthday boy/girl was woken up by my parents and spoilt silly with gifts and hugs. Mummy would make a traditional Malayali meal, including a delicious pal payasam with raisins and cashews. She continues to make payasam on our birthdays even now, although we are in different parts of the world. The difference is that she now has extended her payasam universe to include grandchildren and their spouses. The most recent beneficiary of her payasam was the American husband of my niece who lives in America.

At eighty-four, Mummy continues to live a stubbornly independent life at her home in Kochi. I visit her en route to my constituency, Thiruvananthapuram, looking forward to eating her malakushyam and urulakizhangu upperi. And if she has prepared her signature thakkali pachadi, that is the most perfect meal I can ask for.

I remember how special festivals were in our childhood, especially Vishu, when my parents would wake us up at dawn, keeping their palms on our eyes and leading us to the pooja room where we could open our eyes to see the elaborate Vishu *kani* arrangement. Vishu was also about the entire family getting together for a fabulous sadhya with a variety of traditional dishes and payasams.

By some miracle, I have celebrated the last two Vishus with Mummy and my sisters. During the 2019 elections, Shobha flew down from California to join my election campaign in Thiruvananthapuram, and Smita came down for a few days, so we were able to celebrate Vishu with Mummy, enjoying a grand sadhya. In 2020, one of my sisters, Smita, and my mother were both stuck in Delhi with me during the pandemic 'lockdown', so we got to spend Vishu together with Mummy again. The food was ordered in from Mahabelly, a restaurant in Delhi that serves fantastic Kerala cuisine, and I remember sitting down for a great sadhya with my family. It was like old times all over again. I look forward to many more meals and memories with Mummy in the years to come.

URULAKIZHANGU UPPERI

Ingredients

- 4 medium-sized potatoes
- 2 tbs oil (use coconut or sesame oil for best taste). May add a little more if needed
- 6–8 whole red chillies
- 2 medium-sized red onions
- 1/2 tsp turmeric powder
- Salt to taste

Method

- In a heated pan, sauté onions and red chillies till both are glazed, slightly brown and roasted. Grind this into a paste.
- Wash, peel and chop the potatoes into small, even sized cubes. Toss the chopped potatoes into a skillet or pan, add the onion-chilli paste, sprinkle half a tsp of turmeric and salt to taste. Add enough water to boil the potatoes in the paste.
- Cover the pan and cook on medium or low flame until the potatoes are mostly cooked.

- Remove the lid and roast potatoes on low heat until the water evaporates. If needed, you may add a little more oil. Gently flip the potatoes and roast the other side too on medium heat, for another 2 minutes.

MALAKUSHYAM

Ingredients

- 1 large bunch of finely chopped greens: 1 bunch of spinach or 1/2 bunch of spinach + 1/2 bunch of drumstick leaves
- 1/2 cup tur dal
- 1/2 tsp haldi
- 1/2 cup grated coconut
- 1 tsp whole jeera seeds
- 1 tomato
- Chilli powder to taste
- Salt to taste

Method

- Pressure cook the tur dal with 1/2 tsp haldi.
- Grind the grated coconut along with whole jeera seeds.
- In a separate pan, cook one chopped tomato, haldi, chilli powder and the chopped green leaves.
- Add cooked dal and ground coconut to the cooked greens. Add salt to taste. Add water to make it the right consistency and boil for a couple of minutes.
- Heat 1 tsp coconut oil and toss a whole red chilli, curry leaves and whole cumin. Add to the dal at the end.
- Traditionally malakushyam is made with pumpkin, 'kumblanga', or other marrows, but my memory is of a spinach malakushyam being the family's favourite.

PRAWN PICKLE

Ingredients

- 1 kg shelled prawns
- 125 gm garlic
- 4 onions
- 12 red chillies
- 1/2 tsp peppercorns
- 375 gm gingelly oil
- 375 gm vinegar
- 90 gm ginger
- 1 tsp mustard seeds
- 1 tsp cumin seeds
- 1 tbs turmeric powder
- 10 green chillies
- One sprig curry leaves
- 1 tbs sugar
- Salt to taste

Method

- Grind the onions, red chillies, pepper, 4 cloves of garlic to a smooth paste.
- Put in a saucepan along with the prawns and 2 cups of water and salt. Simmer till all the water evaporates. Remove from the flame.
- Heat half the oil and fry the cooked prawns till nicely browned. Remove from the oil and keep aside.
- Grind half the ginger, half the garlic, mustard seeds, 1 tbs turmeric powder and cumin seeds with 2 tbs of vinegar to form a paste.

- Slice the remaining ginger, garlic and green chillies.
- Add the remaining oil to the oil in which the prawns were fried and fry all the sliced ingredients till aromatic.
- Add the curry leaves and the ground paste and continue to fry, stirring continuously.
- Add the vinegar, season with salt and bring to a boil.
- Now add the fried prawns and sugar and simmer, stirring occasionally till the oil floats to the surface. Cool well and store in airtight jars/bottles.

SHONALI ROHAN RANADE, RADIO JOCKEY

MOTHER: KALPANA MADHUKAR JOSHI

I grew up in a large joint family that lived in a sprawling vada (traditional Maharashtrian-style mansion) in a village in Aurangabad. I remember our family sitting in a circle, cross-legged, in the large courtyard to eat tasty, rustic meals, chatting incessantly and asking for more of the delicious food.

I salivate even today at the memory of one of our breakfast staples: crushed chapattis from the night before, tossed in oil and mixed with a fiery red chilli and garlic thecha and enjoyed with a side of finely chopped onions and fresh coriander leaves.

Living the fast-paced city life today and eating what we city animals eat, I often long for the food that we ate as kids. Looking back, I realize how nutritionally balanced was the food in our Deshasht Brahmin household. There was an abundance of fresh, leafy vegetables in our farms, and the dishes on the menu always included them along with shengdanya che kut (crushed peanuts), til, onions and garlic. There were bhakris and other Indian breads made with a variety of freshly-milled jowar, bajra and other grains and cereals. My grandfather, an Ayurvedic physician, insisted that our meals be wholesome:

varan-bhat, bhaji-poli, koshimbir, chutney, toop (dal rice, vegetable, chapatti/bhakri, a salad, a green chutney and home-made ghee) were a must every day. The chutneys were made from til, flax seeds, peanuts and other seeds and garlic, among other things, all very high on nutritional value.

Aai was a city girl who knew nothing about cooking before she got married and moved to my father's village in Aurangabad. There she was exposed to life in a joint family, cooking in huge quantities and that too on wood-fired chulhas. Everything was different and new for her but she learnt all of it from her mother-in-law and the other women in the family. The men were also foodies and loved to cook. She fondly recalls how she learnt many a family dish from my grandfather who was a passionate cook. In fact, when my parents moved to Aurangabad when I was nearly ten years old, my grandfather accompanied us and would often tell my mother he would cook a meal for all of us. Aai, who had by then taken up a job, would be happy that her father-in-law was not just cooking a great meal for us but was also teaching her two daughters to be independent women.

Aai made a number of delicious dishes that I loved, including gharges, scrumptious sweet pooris made from red pumpkins, bharli shevgyachya shenga, shevgyachya shenganchi saar (a spicy curry of stuffed drumsticks), a sweet and sour bharli karli (stuffed bitter gourd) and a variety of snacks made with multigrain flours. My favourite dish from her kitchen, however, will always remain her kulithpeeth shengole, handmade pasta made from horse gram flour and cooked in a spicy gravy of onions, garlic, red chilli powder and home-made garam masala. This is a dish specific to the Marathwada region where our family hails from, and Aai mastered this under the supervision of my grandmother who was a terrific cook. Every time I visit her in Aurangabad, I request her to cook this for me, but, sadly, I have never managed to cook it on my own.

Aai also made other dishes that I still adore. For instance, her gavhachi kheer, a simple kheer made with soaked, ground wheat and jaggery/sugar, is one of my all-time favourites, as are her khare shankarpale—savoury diamond-shaped fried biscuits, often with additions such as sesame or spinach leaves. Aai also quickly adopted the other rituals of life in the village and mastered the art of making kurdai (thin sundried wheat/jowar/rice-based noodles) and kharodya (bajra/jowar soaked, ground, steamed into small spicy cakes that are sun-dried during peak summer). These were fried and enjoyed during monsoons or year-long, as accompaniment with meals. To this day, I get my supply of kurdai and kharodya from her to enjoy all through the year.

It has been a long time since I left my childhood home and the simple joys of village life behind, but every time I eat an expensive, insipid meal at a restaurant, I think of the lip-smacking dishes that Aai and my uncles and aunts used to cook in their simple kitchen, on a chulha. I long for those authentic, delicious meals. Maybe it was the smoky flavours of the chulha-cooked meals. Maybe it was the love with which the meals were cooked. Or, maybe it was everything combined.

UKADPENDI

Ingredients

- 1 cup wheat flour
- 1 finely chopped onion
- 2–3 green chillies, chopped finely

- Curry leaves
- Small lemon-sized ball of tamarind
- Small piece of jaggery crushed (as per preference)
- 4 to 5 tbs ghee
- Peanuts, coriander leaves and grated coconut for garnishing
- Salt
- Oil for seasoning

Method

- Roast the wheat flour in a pan till it turns pink and take off the flame.
- Put 2 cups of water to boil, and in the meantime, put 2 tbs of oil in a pan and sauté the peanuts, onions, chillies, and add salt to taste.
- Then add the roasted wheat flour, tamarind pulp and jaggery, mix well and add the boiled water to the pan.
- Cover and cook, keeping the flame on simmer.
- Check to make sure the mixture does not burn or stick to the bottom of the pan.
- Remove once done and garnish with grated coconut and coriander leaves.

BHARLI KARLI

Ingredients

- 3–4 bitter gourds
- 3 tsp roasted, crushed peanuts
- 1 tsp sesame, roasted and made into a paste
- 2 tsp crushed/grated copra (dried coconut)
- 1 1/2 tsp roasted gram flour

- 1 tsp onion-garlic masala (available in stores)
- 1/2 tsp salt
- Red chilli powder (as per taste)
- 1/2 tsp turmeric powder
- Juice of half a lemon
- Jaggery to taste

Method

- Wash the bitter gourd, dry and make lengthwise slits to remove the seeds.
- Make sure one side of the gourds is intact since masala has to be stuffed into it.
- Squeeze a lemon over the gourds and sprinkle them with salt. Set them aside for half an hour on a plate that is slightly tilted so that the bitter juice of the gourds can separate.
- Now steam the bitter gourds.
- In the meanwhile, combine crushed peanuts and sesame seeds with copra. Add onion-garlic masala, half a tsp of salt, red chilli powder and turmeric powder to the mixture.
- Stuff this mixture into the steamed gourds.
- Pour 3 tbs oil in a pan, place the stuffed bitter gourds in the hot oil and fry them. Flip them carefully so that the stuffing does not spill out.
- Sprinkle the roasted gram flour on the gourds and add grated jaggery so that it mixes with the gram flour and caramelizes.
- After frying the gourds for about 4 minutes, garnish with grated copra, sesame seeds and coriander leaves.
- This dish is delicious with either jowar/bajra bhakri or chapattis. It never fails to remind me of meals at our wada in the village.

SUDHA MENON, AUTHOR, FOUNDER, GET WRITING AND WRITING WITH WOMEN

MOTHER: PRAMILA RADHAKRISHNAN

Almost four decades since I finished school, I still have vivid memories of rushing home from school early evening, flinging the bag on the sofa and sitting down to eat at the family's rickety dining table. What followed was a ritual practised to perfection: I would pile up my plate with steaming hot rice, then make a depression in the centre of it and pour Amma's spicy drumstick sambar, and crush a few deep-fried pappadams into the plate before polishing off every morsel.

Amma was just sixteen, a young girl living a carefree life in a tiny coastal village in Kerala, when she got married to Acchan and moved to her marital home in Mumbai. It was there that she learnt the rudiments of cooking from her mother-in-law, my acchamma, who taught her Palakkad-style Malayali recipes. She was already familiar with cooking Malappuram style dishes, thanks to a trio of aunts who would cook up a feast at her ancestral home almost every day because they were all foodies.

Growing up with Amma's food was possibly the most exciting part of my childhood in suburban Mumbai, in the early 1970s. And if going to school was the worst kind of punishment for an average student like me, returning home was the best reward because of the goodies that awaited every evening. Our humble home would be full of the aromas of Amma's myriad culinary experiments—if one evening we got to eat spicy, plump Punjabi samosas, another day it would be batata vada, parippu vada or uzhunnu vada.

Amma has always been an instinctive cook, throwing together whatever is available in the kitchen to make delicious meals. Since the better part of our childhood was spent in railway accommodation that always came with a little garden, she grew plenty of stuff that she used in our meals. Freshly plucked red or green amaranth leaves would be turned into a simple mezhukkuvaratti (stir fry) or malakushyam; colocasia leaves would be made into patra/alu wadi (spicy rolls filled with besan) while the stem would be used to make pulingari, a sour dal with tamarind that was perfect with fresh steamed rice.

The tangy pulingari is an incredibly versatile dish that can be made with any vegetable that's available—from the humble ash gourd to red pumpkin, okra or tomato. Amma's love for sour curries meant that this dish was a great part of our growing up years. The pulingari I loved most was the one with soft cooked red pumpkin that lent it a slight sweetness. The best part of the dish was the crunch that came from sprinkling a few fried pappadams over it just before serving it with rice. Ah, bliss.

Summer months always bring back childhood memories of seeing Amma finish up her routine chores early so that she could get down to her favourite task during mango season:

making pickles. The preparation of my favourite variety, kadumanga—fiery, oil-free pickle made from raw baby mangoes—would begin early summer, when the tiny mangoes would make a brief appearance in the market before being snapped up by the south Indian families who lived in our town. Months later, Amma would open the bharani to bring out the baby mangoes swimming in red hot liquid, the perfect accompaniment for rice, curd and pappadam on rainy days.

Amma loved summer despite Mumbai's scorching heat because of the continuous supply of desi varieties of mangoes which she could turn into several kinds of pickles and half a dozen mango dishes that she had learnt from her mother and aunts. Summer was when we got treated to an extraordinary variety of mango curries from Amma's repertoire, some made with raw mangoes, others with ripe mangoes, and each as delicious as the other.

Amma is fiercely proud of these recipes that she says have been passed down the generations. She insists that our Acchan, a great foodie, never enjoyed a fish curry made by anyone else, after having tasted her pomfret and raw mango curry in the early days of their marriage.

Amma's sadhyas, made on Onam and Vishu or special occasions such as birthdays and wedding anniversaries, make me go weak at the knees even now. Nothing can compare to the taste of her pachadi, kootu curry, pulinji, olan and kaalan; to this day these are the flavours I crave when I am away from home. She is ageing now and not able to prepare a full-scale sadhya but insists on making the kaalan and payasam whenever we prepare a family sadhya.

Amma's sweet tooth and her repertoire of desserts are legendary. The divine pazhampori she makes for her grandchildren, the softest unniappams, melt-in-the-mouth rawa ladoos, velvety ela adas, fluffy puran polis and juicy balushahis glistening in sugar syrup coating. I remember once coming back from school to be welcomed with a batch of warm nankhatai that she had persuaded the neighbourhood bakery to bake for her.

I tell her sometimes that her legacy to me is her sweet tooth and her stubborn refusal to let life's knocks defeat her.

AMMA'S AVOLI KOOTAAN WITH
RAW MANGOES AND COCONUT

Ingredients

* 500 gm white pomfret, cleaned and filleted
* 3 green chillies sliced lengthwise
* 1 tsp ginger juliennes
* 1 large raw mango cut into cubes
* 1 cup fresh, grated coconut
* Red chilli powder as per taste
* 4 tsp coriander powder
* 1/4 of an onion, chopped
* 2 sprigs curry leaves
* 2 tsp coconut oil
* Salt to taste

Method

* Cook the fish and raw mangoes together with salt, green chillies, ginger and chilli powder in a pan. Amma uses the traditional *manchatti*—earthenware used for cooking in south Indian homes—and swears these vessels enhance not just the taste but also the nutritional value of food.

- Grind coriander powder, coconut and onion to a fine paste.
- Add to the cooked fish and mango. Simmer for just a minute and remove from the flame.
- Drizzle a tsp of fresh coconut oil and add curry leaves.
- Serve with steaming hot rice. This curry can also be made with mackerel, surmai or prawns.

RAW MANGO AND CUCUMBER CURRY

Ingredients

- 1/4 kg ash gourd/ vellarikka/ drumstick, skinned and chopped
- 2–3 raw mangoes, chopped
- 1/2 coconut, grated
- 3–4 fistfuls of tur dal
- 1 tsp turmeric powder
- 1 tsp cumin seeds
- 3 tsp chilli powder
- 1/2 tsp mustard seeds
- 1/4 tsp fenugreek seeds
- 1 whole red chilli
- 2 sprigs curry leaves
- Salt to taste

Method

- Cook tur dal in a pressure cooker.
- Cook mangoes and cucumber/drumsticks separately with chilli and turmeric powder. Add salt when half cooked. Add the cooked dal to this and allow to simmer until the vegetables are cooked soft.

- Grind coconut with cumin seeds to a fine paste.
- Add to the dal and vegetables and cook till it starts bubbling and frothing.
- Season with whole red chilli, mustard and fenugreek seeds and toss in the curry leaves in the end.
- This dal can also be made with jackfruit seeds peeled, chopped and cooked with the dal and is a delicious summer staple in Kerala homes.
- Serve with rice and pappadam.

RIPE MANGO CHAMMANDI

Ingredients

- 2–3 ripe/raw mangoes
- 4–5 whole red chillies
- 1/4 onion
- 1 tsp coconut oil
- Salt to taste

Method

- Roast the chillies, dice the mangoes and chop the onion. Grind all the ingredients together to a fine paste. Drizzle with coconut oil. Serve with rice/kanjee or even with dosas.

MANGO PULISSERY

Ingredients

- 4–5 ripe mangoes
- 1/2 litre curd

- 1/2 grated coconut
- 4 green chillies, chopped
- 1 tsp cumin seeds
- 4–5 black peppercorns
- 1 tsp of red chilli powder or as per your taste
- 1/4 tsp turmeric powder
- 1/4 tsp mustard seeds
- 1/4 tsp fenugreek seeds
- 2 sprigs curry leaves
- 1 whole dried red chilli
- 1 tsp crushed jaggery
- 1/4 kg chopped yellow cucumber or ash gourd
- Salt to taste

Method

- Grind the coconut, green chillies, cumin and peppercorns to a fine paste.
- Toss the chopped ripe mangoes, yellow cucumber/ash gourd into the cooker with the dried chilli, salt and turmeric powder and a little water and set to cook. Remove from the flame after three whistles, stir gently and then allow to boil on slow flame.
- Add the coconut paste and crushed jaggery to half a litre of beaten sour curd. Mix well and add to the vegetables and allow to simmer on slow flame, stirring to make sure the curd doesn't split.
- Season with mustard, fenugreek, whole red chilli and sprigs of curry leaves.

SUHASINI MANIRATNAM, ACTOR, DIRECTOR

MOTHER: KOMALAM CHARUHASAN

Manni, my mother, was a strict parent and I would often end up in her bad books. At seventeen, I joined a photography class where I was the only girl. She would often get mad at me over this and shout and rant about it, making her displeasure very clear. On days she would be particularly angry and shout at me too much, I would look forward to the evenings because I knew she would prepare my favourite capsicum poriyal before I returned from school. I would tuck into a huge serving, and both of us would go to bed happy, our argument forgotten.

Manni treated me to the same poriyal meal and her signature kesari bhaat the day I won my first National Film Award for best actress. It was a double bonanza for me. Her kesari bhaat is extra special because instead of cashews, which most people use for this dish, she uses soaked almonds. Even now there are days when I crave this preparation.

I grew up in a small village called Paramakudi, near Rameshwaram, in Tamil Nadu. Ours was a joint family and both my father and aththi (grandfather) were lawyers.

It was a typical Iyengar household and we ate Iyengar food at home, made by Akka (grandma) and Manni. My mother had lost her own mother very early in life, so she learnt everything about cooking from her mother-in-law.

As a household, we were not fussy about food, but the elders were very particular about hygiene and outside food was not allowed. It was such a strict household that even betel leaves or betel nuts weren't allowed in the house. Everyone talks about the importance of washing hands because of COVID-19 today, but it was the norm in our house all those decades ago. Everybody had to wash their hands and feet before entering the house. I remember Akka would insist that even the back of our feet had to be washed because it was believed that Yama, the God of death, came into the house stealthily, on the back of our feet and heels!

In Iyengar homes of those days, there was no tradition of eating 'breakfast'. It was always a proper, big brunch of sambar, rice, vegetables and salad at 9 a.m., after which we rushed to school. My father and aththi left for court right after and returned around 4 p.m. Manni would always have tiffin waiting for them because they usually skipped lunch. Tiffin would typically be upma, dosai or pooris, and we kids ate this upon returning from school too.

Dinner was at 6 p.m., and everybody had to finish their meal by 6.30 p.m. so that we could catch the evening show at the village cinema at 6.45 p.m. Aththi was very fond of movies, and we would all go trooping after him to the cinema, with much excitement.

We would usually have rasam, rice, dal and a vegetable for dinner. Manni always had a reason for making us eat different vegetables. For instance, okra was prepared quite frequently because it was good for the brain and would help us do well in maths. And all sorts of beans had to be eaten for overall wellness and good health.

We children dreaded the visit of one of our aunts who lived in Madras because her arrival meant that we had to eat a lot of vegetables. Mealtimes would include a series of rice dishes— aubergine and rice or cauliflower and rice—and by the time we finished, we would have no space in our tummies for sambar and rasam, which, she said, had no nutrition anyway. It was torture and we would look forward to her departure!

Manni had a number of specialties that we all loved as kids. Her parippu usili—she usually made it with banana blossom or beans—was a great hit. She also excelled in preparing another Iyengar staple, morkozhambu, which was so good that she had her brood eating out of her hand.

When special guests were expected, she would make her signature arachu vitta sambar with pearl onions. While most Iyengar homes make everyday sambar with a dry sambar powder that is stocked in the larder, the arachu vitta sambar calls for a freshly ground masala with fried coconut. She would roast whole spices such as coriander and red chillies along with grated coconut till the entire house was filled with the spicy aroma. The perfect accompaniment to this was a potato fry that the kids absolutely loved. I still remember hanging around to watch the potatoes fry in the hot oil, gradually going from white to yellow and then turning a fiery red and almost shiny, with the coating of oil. Some of the pieces would get caramelized and almost burn, sticking to the bottom of the pan. These were the tastiest, if we could manage to scrape them off.

There is another vivid memory of Manni and Akka sitting down to clean and peel banana blossoms for a delicious dish. The process had us kids spellbound as one of them would peel back layer after layer of the blossom to find the tenderest part or its heart. It was tedious and required patience, but when you got to the centre, it was a thing of beauty and tasted divine; sometimes Manni or Akka would let us have a tiny bit of it, which we would share and relish.

Life back then was simple but brimming with excitement about everyday things in the house. I remember how much I enjoyed when white butter was made at home. The women of the household would remove the top layer of curd each day and keep it away in a vessel in a dark, cool corner of the kitchen. After a few days, Manni would settle down in a corner of the kitchen, away from the hustle and bustle, to churn the butter. Cold water would be kept in a vessel near her, and as she churned, the cream would gradually form little balls which she would toss into the water. Sometimes she would give into our pleas and allow us kids a chance to churn the cream for a few minutes. It was fascinating to see the entire thing eventually forming a big white ball of butter that would float magnificently on the surface of the water. Once it was done, Manni would line up the girls of the house and slather the leftover butter on our skin, telling us it was the best moisturizer in the world. I loved feeling the butter slide over my skin, and even today, that is how I keep my skin supple. This is not the end of the butter story. Manni would then put the butter in a pan and heat it up, sending us to the garden to fetch either moringa or curry leaves that were added to the pan so that the ghee would not have any bitterness from the butter. When the ghee was done and taken out of the pan, we would wait for Manni to make our special treat. She would simply add rice flour and sugar into the pan and mix it up to form an instant dessert, which was so delicious that we would scoop it right off the hot pan and devour it.

Tea time tiffin was great in our house; Manni would treat us to upma kozhukattai, pooris and bhajjis made from aubergines, onions and raw plantains. When my father started making more money, she started making cauliflower bhajjis, which were a luxury. Later, when my son was growing up, Manni took to treating him and her other grandchildren to paneer bhajjis. I never even knew in my growing up years that paneer could be used for anything other than rasagollas.

Diwali breakfast was always the softest idlis and vadais with sambar and chutney and delicious chakkara pongal. The thayir vadais (dahi vadas) in our house were unbelievably good and guests relished them when they came to exchange greetings during festivals.

When it came to festivities, Manni always kept the meals modest because we coexisted with an economically backward community where even eating rice every day was a luxury for many of our neighbours. Most of them lived on bajra, and Manni felt it was unfair to have sumptuous meals when the rest of them had nothing special on their plates. The dessert we got to have often was a kanji made with moong dal, jaggery and milk, because she said poor people got to have payasam only once a year, so how could we eat it all year round? When Manni made this kanji, the aroma would waft across to their homes. They would come over eagerly, and she would feed all of us happily. Our house was open to everyone because the elders believed in sharing whatever was available to us. She also made the best rawa and besan ladoos but these were for rare occasions.

The girls of the house learnt to make jalebi, which was a regular dessert, and I learnt to make the perfect south Indian murukku and Manni's diamond biscuits—the savoury version as well as the sweet version dipped in sugar syrup. These were our favourite instant snacks that Manni made during our childhood and they disappeared into our tummies as soon as they were made!

Even at eighty-five, Manni's passion for cooking remains undiminished, and there are days I become her little girl all over again and sit back to enjoy a meal that she cooks for the family.

CAPSICUM PORIYAL

Ingredients for dry roasting

- A few red chillies
- 2 tsp coriander seeds
- A pinch of hing
- Salt as per taste
- Oil to sauté

Other ingredients

- 6 to 7 capsicums
- 2 tsp roasted Bengal gram
- 1/2 tsp mustard seeds for seasoning

Method

- Cut the capsicum into long slices.
- After dry roasting the ingredients, add 2 tsp of roasted Bengal gram and powder it evenly—not too fine and not too coarse.
- In a kadhai, add 2 to 3 tsp of oil (capsicum does not need much oil), add mustard seeds and when they start

to splutter, add the cut capsicum and salt and sauté it
well.

• When done, add the coarse powder and stir only for one
minute and the poriyal is ready to eat.

VAAZHAIPOO PARUPPU USILI

Ingredients

• 1 banana blossom, peeled, cut into pieces and soaked in
watered down, thin buttermilk.
• 2 cups tur dal
• 4–5 red chillies
• A pinch of hing
• Salt to taste
• 3 tsp oil

Method

• Soak tur dal for half an hour.
• Chop and boil the banana blossom with salt. Strain the
water and keep aside.
• Grind the tur dal coarsely with chillies, salt and hing.
• Mix the ground dal with the banana blossom and steam
cook for 10 minutes either in an idli steamer or any
ordinary steaming vessel.
• Next, in a kadhai, pour oil, add mustard seeds, and when
they start to splutter, add the dal and banana blossom
mixture and cook on a low flame.
• In a few minutes, the tur dal mixture will be ready to serve
with rice or on its own, as a main course.

KESARI

Ingredients

* 1 cup rawa (semolina)
* 2 cups sugar
* A little under 3 cups of water
* Cardamoms (elaichi)
* Pachcha karpooram (cooking camphor)
* Cashews as per preference
* 1/2 cup ghee
* Kesari (saffron colour)

Method

* Fry cashews in ghee and keep aside.
* Boil water in a separate vessel.
* In a kadhai, fry rawa in some ghee. Once melted, the ghee should cover the rawa.
* Once the rawa is roasted golden, pour the boiling water on it so it cooks well and remains moist.
* Make sure the rawa has no lumps when cooked.
* Add sugar and stir well so it dissolves and integrates with the rawa.
* Add kesari colour, elaichi and a pinch of pachcha karpooram. Add the roasted cashews and put off the flame.
* Add a bit more ghee if the kesari seems dry.

TISCA CHOPRA, ACTOR

MOTHER: PAMMI ARORA

I am not sure how old I was in this memory, but we were living in Kabul where my father was posted those days and I was young enough to insist that I wanted a cake with an entire farm house on it for my birthday. I still remember my excitement when Mum surprised me with the exact cake I had dreamt of! It was incredible: at the centre of the cake was a tiny cottage with creepers on the walls and all around was a garden with trees, animals roaming around and a cute picket fence. It was so beautiful that I could not bring myself to cut and eat it. That remains one of my most cherished memories because my mother made the cake from scratch in freezing weather, simply because she wanted to make me feel special.

Kabul was an entirely different world from the one she was familiar with. She grew up in Punjab, later Shimla and other places where fruits and vegetables were aplenty. But when she found herself in distant Kabul, where it was rare to see shoots of green come out of the earth because of the biting cold, she quickly adjusted to that too.

I still remember the smallest things about our life there. There were hardly any Indian ingredients and not many vegetables grew in the minus 20 degrees Celsius cold. So my mother largely raised us on continental food—roast chicken, mutton, tinned sardines and veggies that grew in harsh winters, such as brussels sprouts.

Mum comes from a family of passionate foodies who routinely innovate in the kitchen. She did that in Kabul too, learning to use the summers to make and freeze rotis that we pulled out and heated on a hot plate (no microwaves back then!). I remember the large number of cocktail samosas she would make and pop into the freezer, to be used when we entertained. Kabul was a very social place. The few Indian families that lived there met regularly—for Diwali there would sometimes be six parties, plus the feasts for Eid and Holi, all joyous and fun-filled. Mum loved entertaining and meeting people and was a generous host, swinging into action much ahead of the party and making sure there was enough food to feed an army. Mum has an innate talent for cooking and can pair the most unlikely ingredients to make a memorable dish.

I cannot imagine how she managed on her own in an alien country, catering entire meals for as many as forty people, making paneer dishes, a variety of snacks, including her popular cocktail samosas, and dessert, all of which disappeared within the hour of our guests arriving!

My parents missed eating Indian food so much that it was a treat for them when Indian families returning to Kabul from India carried bundles of spinach or tender bhindi (okra) as gifts. Mum would cook up an Indian meal to celebrate and would be aghast when my brother and I would turn up our noses and refused to eat the bhindi subzi. 'But it is from India and it is so rare to get,' she would say and would be miffed when we did not share her excitement about it. To this day, I have a healthy aversion to bhindi and won't eat it if given a choice.

Later, when we returned to India, festivals in our household were no longer grand because Mum started working too and time was at a premium. Since we were a family of dessert lovers, Mum ensured we had enough dessert to fix our cravings. The problem was that because she was such a good cook, we never wanted any store-bought desserts. In addition to Indian desserts such as sevaiyan and halwa, we had a range of unconventional desserts too. If anyone gifted us a box of barfi, Mum would reinvent it, using it to create a layered cake, on which she would pour some crush or sauce and make a delicious new dessert of it.

In Kabul, we had access to the extensive stock at the American commissary and dessert at home would therefore be rather exotic for those times. We would have desserts made of ingredients such as strawberry compote, blueberry crush and cranberry juice. I still remember this heavenly dessert she made just once—a layered dessert with oranges soaked in their own juice, put together with grated coconut and biscuits. The problem is that when we ask her to make it today, she has no clue how to. 'I would just use all the good stuff in the fridge to make an impromptu dessert for us!' she says.

Mum is from a Sikh family, who are joyous eaters. She can look at a cut of meat or just touch a fish and know exactly how to cook it. My favourites from her kitchen are her kaale chane, kale gaajar ki kanji and besan wale lotus stem. These are outstanding. And I can never have enough of her lassi. She elevates this simple drink to another level altogether, adding mint, roasted cumin and aamchur powder. When I visit her in Delhi, where she lives with Dad, I look forward to having this and her wadiwaali aloo, both of which always remind me of home.

Now that I too am a mother, I know the efforts she took to cook tasty, nourishing meals for us. When I was a teenager, I remember she would keep up a steady commentary from the kitchen while making a dish, telling me exactly what ingredients she was adding and why. She insisted that I know enough cooking to be independent and put me in charge of Sunday dinner for the family. All of that came handy during the three-month lockdown during the COVID-19 pandemic when I found myself making the things she cooked at home— shimla mirch subzi, kurkure bhindi, kaale chane, etc.

When it comes to food, presentation is a very important part of the process for my mother. Our desserts, pulaos and raitas always had garnishes of nuts, seeds or freshly chopped herbs and masalas. I was chatting with her one day during the lockdown and she suggested I make a butterfly-shaped paratha for my daughter. I decided to use that idea to surprise my little girl. I was putting the final touches to the laboriously made paratha when she called from Delhi to suggest that I could use black peppercorns for the butterfly's eyes! Needless to say, my daughter was delighted with her surprise lunch, even though I had some trouble getting her to eat her beautiful paratha.

My mother and I both like rice very much and when we meet, we both enjoy a meal of rice with a nice gravy, a crispy vegetable, such as lotus stem with besan, and a chutney. That is my idea of a perfect meal made by Mom.

WADIWAALI ALOO

Ingredients

- 1/2 piece Punjabi urad dal wadi (available in many grocery stores)
- 1 tbs ghee or oil
- A pinch of asafoetida
- 1 tsp cumin seeds
- 1/2 tsp turmeric powder

* 1 tsp coriander powder
* 1/2 tsp red chilli powder
* 1/2 tsp cumin powder
* 4 medium size potatoes boiled, peeled and cubed
* 2 medium tomatoes made into a paste
* 2 medium onions made into a paste
* Salt to taste
* 1 tsp each ginger and garlic paste
* Fresh coriander leaves for garnishing

Method

* Heat oil or ghee and add cumin seeds and asafoetida.
* Add onion paste and roast till golden in colour and then add ginger-garlic paste, stirring well before adding tomato paste and cumin, coriander, chilli, turmeric powders and salt. Mix well.
* To this, add the wadi broken into small pieces and stir till well coated.
* Cook for five minutes and add cubed potatoes, stirring well before adding water to boil till the dish gets slightly thick.
* Switch off the gas and add a tsp of garam masala (optional).
* Garnish with coriander leaves and serve with steamed rice or parathas.

LOTUS STEM WITH BESAN

Ingredients

* 1 lotus stem sliced on the slant into 1/4-inch pieces
* 75 gm besan

- 3 tsp coriander powder
- 2 tsp chilli powder or as preferred
- Salt to taste
- 1 tsp aamchur (dried mango powder)
- 2 tbs ghee or oil
- Coriander leaves for garnishing
- 4–5 tsp oil
- Salt to taste

Method

- Clean and pressure cook the lotus stem till tender. This usually takes 10–12 minutes.
- When cool, open the cooker and toss the water in which it was cooked.
- Dry roast the besan in a kadhai till it turns light golden brown.
- Add salt, coriander powder, chilli powder to taste, and 1 tsp aamchur powder and mix well.
- Add 2 tbs of ghee or oil to this besan mix and stir rapidly to avoid formation of lumps. Add the lotus stem to this.
- Mix well so that all the pieces of the lotus stem are coated with the besan masala.
- Sprinkle some water over it to make sure the coating process is complete.
- Put off the flame when cooked, garnish with coriander leaves and serve as a side dish with rice or parathas.

UDAY KOTAK, EXECUTIVE
VICE-CHAIRMAN AND MANAGING
DIRECTOR, KOTAK MAHINDRA BANK

MOTHER: INDIRA SURESH KOTAK

Growing up in a large joint family of sixty people in Babulnath, south Bombay, I was the pampered eldest grandchild on whom everyone doted. My earliest food memory of those times include the fabulous puran polis that my mother used to make. In fact, they were so delicious that I would insist on having them every day. This was not easy because in joint families of those days, the elder women of the house, along with the cook, fixed the menu for the entire week in advance, and it could not change for a little boy who threw tantrums.

My mother, however, found a way around this with an innovative idea. Mohanthaal, a Gujarati sweet made with besan, sugar and ghee, was offered as prasad to the deities in our home every day. When I would ask for puran polis, Mummy would simply take some of the mohanthaal, heat it up with milk, thicken it and stuff it into my rotis. I was too little then to realize the difference between puran polis that Gujaratis stuff with tuvar dal and mohanthaal which is made with besan. I happily ate the puran polis and also took some to school for a snack. It was not until much later that I realized my mother's small trick to keep me happy without upsetting the family's set rhythm.

When my grandfather moved to set up a home of his own in Gamdevi, along with my parents, my ba (grandmother) and Mummy took charge of the kitchen, and my puran poli treats became more regular.

Decades later, puran poli continues to be my favourite and my family knows how I like it: thick, with plenty of stuffing in it. The difference between my childhood days and now, of course, is that now I have to watch my portions; I get not more than a half or three quarters of a puran poli to relish because my wife, Pallavi, keeps a watchful eye on my consumption of sweets.

My family originally came from Rajkot, from the region of Kathiawad in north Gujarat, and the food we cooked and served in our joint family reflected that.

One of my favourite combinations from the typical Kathiawadi fare was adad ni dal (urad dal) and meetho bhaath (sweet rice) that Mummy would treat us to once a month, on a Saturday. We relished it with spicy lasun (garlic) chutney, another staple from Kathiawad. Pallavi, who hails from Surat, has learnt this recipe from Mummy, and prepares it for us occasionally and the pleasure of eating that familiar dish from my childhood is immense.

Ringna na olo, the Gujarati version of baingan bharta, is another favourite. This is a mealtime staple in Kathiawadi homes during cold winters, when the baingan is roasted over coal fire, peeled and the pulp cooked. In our house, we sautéed green garlic and green onions in groundnut oil and added no other spice to it. All the flavour in the olo came from the combination of the fresh green garlic and onions. Even today a good meal for me includes ringna no olo and bajra no rotlo.

Mummy also regularly made a meal of watana-batata subzi (green peas and potatoes) served with roti, followed by a delicious moong dal khichdi, with fragrant amba mohr rice, and kadhi. It was the perfect meal, Kathiawadi style, something I continue to cherish.

When I look back, there are some food memories that stand out vividly in my mind. When I would come home from school or from a game of cricket at Oval Maidan, Mummy or Ba would have tall glasses of cold milk with cut fruit ready for me. I could have any amount of this doodh-fruit because it was delicious and also because, back in those days, I dreamt of becoming a cricketer, and I was told doodh-fruit would build up my stamina. During mango season, Mummy would cut the sweetest, tastiest Alphonso mangoes into tiny pieces and add them to milk, and I would easily devour a couple of glasses of it. I continue to have a fondness for doodh-fruit and strawberries with powdered sugar sprinkled on top. Mummy would get strawberries from Mahabaleshwar, wash and chop them up and sprinkle them with powdered sugar.

Come summer and our house would be full of mangoes and aam ras was a given at most meals. But I had my own preference for aam ras. I would only eat it if it was made from tangy, sweet paayari mangoes and not the haapus, which I found too sweet. While most traditional Gujarati homes eat aam ras with padvali rotis—layered rotis—we would have it with phulkas. Mummy knew I loved my aam ras a bit runny and with nothing added to it, not even sugar.

Festival days, when family and friends visited us, was when home-made shrikhand was served with finely diced fruits that gave a nice crunch to the creamy dessert. Ba and Mummy would add fruits such as oranges, bananas and pomegranates to the shrikhand, taking the taste to another level altogether. Puran poli was also a Diwali favourite, so you know where my obsession with this comes from.

They say our mothers lay the early foundation on which we build our dreams and lives. This holds true for me. I have vivid memories of Mummy coming to my school, Hindi Vidya Bhavan, every day, with hot lunch packed in a tiffin box, and she would make sure I ate everything in it. I think I benefitted not just from the nutritious lunch she carried but also from all the love and affection she poured into what she prepared for me.

KATHIAWADI HOME-STYLE 'MITHO BHAAT'

Ingredients

- 2 cups rice
- 1 cup grated jaggery
- 1 cup water
- 2 tbs ghee
- 1 bay leaf
- 2 cinnamon sticks
- 3–4 cloves
- 3–4 cardamoms

Method

- Wash and soak the rice in water for 15 minutes.
- Meanwhile, heat the water and add the grated jaggery. Stir it till the jaggery is completely dissolved. Switch off the gas.
- Drain the rice in a colander.

- Heat 4 tbs of ghee in a pan and add bay leaf, cinnamon sticks, cloves and cardamoms.
- Add the drained rice and stir, making sure each grain is coated with ghee.
- Now add the jaggery water, cover and cook for 10 minutes on a medium flame.
- Our mitho bhaat is ready to be served with adad dal!

GUJARATI-STYLE ADAD NI DAL

Ingredients

- 1 cup urad dal (husked split black lentils)
- 1/2 cup whisked yoghurt, preferably sour
- 2 tsp oil
- 1/2 tsp cumin seeds
- 1/4 tsp asafoetida
- 1 sprig of curry leaves
- 1 tsp garlic paste
- Green chilli paste, as per taste
- 1/2 tsp turmeric powder
- 2 tbs chopped coriander to garnish
- Salt to taste

Method

- Clean, wash and soak the urad dal in enough water in a bowl for 15 minutes. Drain.
- In a pressure cooker, pour 1 1/2 cups of water and add the drained dal and cook for 3 whistles with salt. Allow the cooker to cool before opening the lid.

- Add yoghurt and 1 1/2 cups of water to the cooked dal and mix well. Keep aside.
- Heat oil in a heavy-bottomed pan, add cumin seeds, asafoetida and curry leaves and sauté for a few seconds.
- Add garlic paste, green chilli paste, turmeric powder and the dal-yoghurt mixture and cook for 3–4 minutes, stirring constantly to ensure the dal doesn't stick to the bottom of the pan.
- Switch off the gas. Garnish with chopped coriander leaves.
- Serve piping hot with mitho bhaat!

PURAN POLI

Ingredients for the stuffing

- 1 cup tuvar dal (split pigeon peas)
- 1 1/2 cups water
- 1 1/2 cups grated jaggery

For the dough

- 2 cups whole wheat flour
- 2 tbs oil
- 1 cup water

Method

- Wash and pressure cook the tuvar dal with 1 1/2 cups of water for up to 3–4 whistles. Allow it to cool.
- Knead the dough by mixing oil in the atta and adding water as required. The dough should be soft to the touch.

Smear it with some more oil and cover with a wet cloth or a utensil and let it rest for 20 minutes.

For the stuffing

- Heat 2 tbs ghee in a non-stick pan and add the well-cooked dal.
- Add 1 1/2 cups of grated jaggery and stir continuously, ensuring nothing sticks to the bottom of the pan.
- Add 1/2 tsp cardamom powder and some saffron dissolved in warm water.
- Mix the stuffing well. It should be of a consistency with which you can make balls of 2 inches each.
- Now make about 15 balls from the dough.
- Take one ball of the dough and roll it out on a wooden patla or chakla (flat wooden rolling board) to about 4–5 inches and place one ball of the stuffing in the centre.
- Fold the roti like you do when you make aloo paratha and roll out the poli about 6–7 inches in diameter.
- It should be thick with the stuffing. Cook on a hot griddle on both sides till pink spots appear on the surface.
- Once it balloons up, take it off the tawa/griddle and smear it with copious amounts of ghee and serve hot!

VIDYA BALAN, ACTOR

MOTHER: SARASWATHY BALAN

My sister, Priya, and I grew up with south Indian food cooked at home by Amma. Unlike many mothers, Amma neither had a great liking for cooking nor did she have a bank of recipes handed to her by her own mom. My grandma passed away when Amma was very young, and thus, her only connection with cooking was seeing the family prepare the meals. But to me, good food is all about Amma's cooking.

Everybody in our family has a sweet tooth. This inevitably meant that when we want to celebrate anything special at home, the first thing we think of is the dessert. During my childhood, the highlight of Sunday lunch would be Amma's special treat for us, vella payar, a delicious dessert made by simply cooking moong or red eyed beans with jaggery and coconut till it all came together into a glorious mass. On the days Amma did not make this, Appa would step in with his signature pazham nurukku, steamed yellow bananas cooked in jaggery syrup and ghee, a dish with which he could have my sister and I eating out of his hands. He recently visited his nephews in the US and had everyone licking their fingers in delight when he prepared this dish for them.

I have always had a soft corner for food. I remember, as a kid, the first thing I would do on waking up was rush to the kitchen to select the fruit I would eat as soon as I had brushed my teeth! I waited for my birthday so that Amma would pamper me with my favourite semiya payasam. For the auspicious day of Vishu, she made chakka payasam, a delectable dessert that most Kerala homes make during jackfruit season, with home-made jackfruit preserve, jaggery and dollops of ghee. On Onam, Vishu and other festivals, she also cooked the traditional staples—her avial and mor kootan (Kerala-style kadhi made with curd and coconut) are incomparable, as is her pachadi.

Even years after marriage and setting up home, I have not bothered to train my cooks to prepare Amma's dishes. Palakkad Iyer cooking is very distinct, and I think only years of practice can make it perfect. I am lucky that my parents stay very close to my house and on days that I am not shooting or occupied with work, I still get to eat all my Amma's staples. In fact, I call in advance and tell her to keep my favourite food ready. What I love about her kitchen is that there is always idli-dosa batter ready in the fridge waiting to be relished with her fiery molagapodi. I can make a meal out of molagapodi alone and can eat it in so many ways, even just sprinkled on steaming hot rice with ghee. I also look forward to relishing her sambar made with pearl onions even though it is very rarely prepared these days because peeling them is tedious.

I have a peculiar habit when it comes to food: I can make a meal out of just dry subzi; I don't need roti, rice, bread or even dal to complete a meal. Growing up, Amma would sometimes cook for both meals together when she had to go out for chores and did not have time to cook in the evening. To the great annoyance of my sister, I would come home from school and polish off the entire subzi in just one sitting.

In fact, Amma's home-made pav bhaji without the pav is instant comfort food for me as is her adai—thick pancakes made with a variety of lentils, fiery whole red chillies and curry leaves. This dish is not just tasty, but full of nutrition. The world has discovered multigrain food just now, but we Malayalis have been eating multigrain dishes forever!

Palakkad Iyers have a weakness for everything *puli* or tart and for vellam or jaggery. We use jaggery in everything from kozhukattai—steamed rice balls filled with a mixture of jaggery and grated coconut—payasam and avil or sweetened beaten rice. I remember, back in my childhood, when there was nothing sweet to eat after lunch, Dad would break a coconut and we would enjoy slices of it with jaggery.

One of my most favourite Amma specialities remains theratipal or milk cake made from curdled milk. As kids, we would wait for the milk in the house to curdle and then she would add sugar and caramelize the mixture, reducing it on a low flame till it became a quarter of the quantity. My sister and I would squabble over who would get one spoonful more or less of the delicacy. Today I largely stay off milk, but if this is being prepared at home, rarely as it is, I still have a bit of it and become a child all over again.

Amma's food was also the highlight of travels as kids. The day we had to travel, Amma would get up early to make a big batch of idlis, which she would then dip in molagapodi mixed with oil and cut them neatly into four pieces. She would then make individual packets of three idlis per person and hand it over to us once we were in the train and it was time for lunch. Even now I eat idli the way she made it back then—generously smeared with molagapodi on both sides.

When I was in the third grade, the family went on a long train journey with my aunt and her family and it remains one of my most cherished memories. We went to so many places—Mantralaya, Kumbakonam, Chidambaram, Palakkad, Mangalore, Guruvayoor—and the highlight of the journey was the amazing food. There were parippu vadais with coconut chutney, thayir shadam and all types of fried goodies.

Growing up in a south Indian family is also about loving a lot of chutneys and condiments, including the tart and glorious chamandi podi—tamarind pounded with spices and roasted coconut—that can be eaten with rice, kanji or as an accompaniment to just about anything. Then there is an array of pickles too. My paternal aunt would make kadu manga— a spicy raw baby mango pickle—while Amma's speciality was avakkai, both great when eaten with rice, pappadam or thayir shaadam. Today I can't bring myself to eat bottled pickles because I am addicted to their pickles stored in earthen *bharnis* and bursting with rustic flavours.

I will never forget the excitement around Diwali, growing up in the bylanes of Chembur where entire buildings would come alive with the aromas of a dozen different sweets being made. Diwali specials at our home included Amma's boondi ladoo made under the supervision of a neighbouring mami who was an expert in it. Diwali was truly a community celebration back then because groups of housewives went to each other's homes to help them make the sweet of their choice. Amma's coconut burfi was my favourite thing to eat during Diwali and even now, I look forward to her Diwali sweets with great gusto.

SARASHWATHY BALAN'S PALAKKAD IYER RECIPES

MATTHAN PACHADI

Ingredients

- 350 gm red pumpkin, cubed
- Lemon-sized ball of tamarind soaked and the juice squeezed out
- 1/2 a coconut, grated
- 1 1/2 tsp of jaggery or as per taste
- 2 each, red and green chillies
- 1/2 tsp mustard
- 1/2 tsp turmeric
- Salt to taste

Method

- Cook the pumpkin in tamarind juice with turmeric and jaggery.
- Grind the coconut, mustard seeds and chillies to a fine paste.
- When the pumpkin is cooked, add the ground coconut mixture. Add water as preferred, but the pachadi is medium thick in consistency.
- Season with mustard seeds and whole red chillies, using a tsp of coconut oil.
- Serve with steaming hot rice, pickle and pappadum.

VELLA PAYAR

Ingredients

- 500 gm small red-eyed beans or whole moong

- 400 gm jaggery. Buy jaggery that has a deeper red colour
- 1/4 coconut, grated
- 8–9 cardamoms, powdered
- 2–3 tsp of ghee

Method

- Roast the beans or moong till well toasted, then wash it. Pressure cook (2 whistles) and then cook for another 10 minutes on a low flame.
- The beans/moong must be well-cooked.
- In a heavy bottomed kadhai, add the jaggery which has been grated or chopped into small pieces.
- Add a small quantity of water to melt the jaggery. When melted, add the cooked beans/moong and boil till the water evaporates.
- Switch off the gas and add the grated coconut and cardamom powder. Pour the ghee over the dish and serve hot.

ADAI

Ingredients

- 2 glasses boiled rice
- 1/2 glass tuvar dal
- 1/4 glass whole urad dal
- 4–5 whole red chillies
- 1 heaped tsp cumin seeds
- 1 heaped tsp whole black pepper
- Curry leaves to taste
- Salt to taste

Method

- Soak the rice and dal for 3 hours along with cumin seeds, red chillies, pepper and curry leaves.
- After 3 hours, drain the water and grind to a coarse paste with salt.
- Spread the batter on a heated tawa and make medium thick adais, using til oil.
- Serve hot with a dollop of white butter and some grated jaggery.

MOLGAPODI

Ingredients

- 1 glass of urad dal
- 1/4 glass chana dal
- 2 handfuls white til
- 20 red chillies or as preferred
- 3/4 tsp hing
- Salt to taste

Method

- Roast urad dal and chana dal in a tsp of oil till they turn reddish in colour. Remove from pan and quickly roast the red chillies till crisp.
- Remove from the flame and add hing to the dal and chillies. Add salt and mix well.
- When cool, grind in the mixer, making sure remains coarse.
- Mix either with coconut or til oil and serve with adai, idlis or dosas. Can be also mixed with home-made ghee to make it extra special.

V.R. FEROSE, SENIOR VICE PRESIDENT AND HEAD, SAP ACADEMY FOR ENGINEERING

MOTHER: FATHIMA RASHEED

Growing up in Kharagpur, West Bengal, where my father worked for the South Eastern Railways, my childhood memories are inextricably woven with images of Umma (mother) in the kitchen, cooking up new and exciting recipes that she learnt from other mothers in the railway colony where we lived. It was a diverse community. The twenty families that lived there hailed from different parts of the country. Umma got the recipes from the other women when they chatted at the common well at the centre; we did not have piped water in the house.

She would take great pride in writing down the new recipes she had learnt from her friends and preparing the items forthwith. My maternal grandfather, a foodie himself, would often purchase cookbooks and send them to Umma. If she saw an interesting recipe in a magazine, she would immediately buy it and promptly prepare the dish. Umma, who knew only Kerala staples such as rasam, sambar, aviyal and green vegetables, started making Maharashtrian staples, such as poha and sabudana khichdi, and Bengali dishes, like luchi, aloo fry and khichdi, etc., after she got married. Umma had a way with cooking and rarely did her kitchen experiments disappoint her two boys. She had one ground rule in the house: every meal was freshly cooked, and we had to finish everything by dinner because she did not like to keep leftovers for the next day.

I must have been around eight years old then, and those are some of the most memorable years of my life. The entire community looked forward to Eid because they knew Umma would pull out all the stops to treat everybody to a veritable feast. Umma's preparation for Eid started weeks in advance when she would start getting snacks and sweets ready to distribute to the entire colony. On the day of Eid, biryani, of course, was the highlight of the meal, and I won't be exaggerating if I say that many of our parents' friends waited the entire year to savour my mother's cooking. For dessert, we had three choices: semiya payasam, boondi ladoo and cake. Needless to say, all three were equally delicious. Her cakes were my favourite, and I am delighted that these days she has picked up that passion again, making cakes with dates and persimmons that have everyone in the house drooling. She has always been a payasam lover and extended her experimenting there too. One of my favourites is a very unique payasam she makes with jackfruit seeds.

My favourites from Umma's dizzying array of dishes were the simplest ones, but they could never be replicated by anyone else. Maybe that is what '*maa ke haath ka khana*' is all about—a taste that is unique to every mother's hands. It is difficult to pick one item because my favourites always seemed to come in pairs: puttu with kadala (steamed rice cakes with black chickpeas curry); kanji with payar (rice porridge with green moong curry); dosa with sambar; kappa with chamandhi (steamed tapioca roots with chutney); chapatti with chana dal; coconut rice with egg curry; and many more. For me, the side dish was often the star—the chutney was the most important part of the kappa; the kadala of the puttu; the payar of the kanji; the chana dal of the chapatti; and the sambar of the dosa. In our home, one could ask for repeats of the main dish but never of the side dish. Umma would laugh when I would tell her to serve me a generous portion of the side dish and not underestimate my ability to finish every bit of it.

Since I come from a Muslim family, most people assume that we are primarily meat eaters. But our family largely had vegetarian meals. Fish was a weekend delicacy and mutton and chicken were reserved for special occasions. I do not enjoy non-vegetarian food and sometimes regret missing out on some of Umma's amazing meat dishes. But I did enjoy the coconut rice-egg curry combo that is a staple in many Kerala Muslim homes. While I ate the coconut rice with Umma's egg curry, the rest of the family ate it with meat curry. Pappadams, a salad and pickle were accompaniments to this tasty meal.

Like most kids, I too had a phase when I cribbed often and loudly about Umma's predictable food. Every night I would ask her what she would cook the next day, and she would promise to make something I liked to carry to school for lunch. My recognition and appreciation of the efforts she made to keep us well fed grew considerably when I started living on my own. Even a simple sandwich she made would be delicious, and I often wondered why, when I tried to make the same thing, it did not taste as good. When I started working and living alone, I often thought of the sumptuous breakfasts she would prepare for us because most days I had no time to prepare breakfast and even an omelette and toast seemed like a luxury.

Umma had food for all occasions. When I was sick, she would transform herself into a doctor, knowing exactly what nourishment I needed to ensure quick recovery. The food was both delicious and healthy; rice khichdi and payar with kanji were her cure for every illness and they were my favourite 'sick food'. When I send my kid off to school now with a packed lunch, I often find myself thinking of the variety of snacks she packed in my tiffin box that made me the envy of all my friends. She would sometimes pack vadas for lunch, and I remember how proud I would be when my friends would beg me to share with them. The vadas still make me drool and I wait for Umma to visit me so that I can have my fill of it.

Umma continues to be a passionate cook and feeder of everyone she meets. It is impossible to maintain a controlled diet when she is around. When we were kids, she would constantly hover around us or our guests to ensure that our plates were never empty. Sometimes, it felt like a gentle tug of war—us trying to convince her that we were full and her trying to convince us we were not! I suppose that was her way of showing love. The first Malayalam word that my Maharashtrian wife, Deepali, learnt was 'kazhicho' (which translates to 'did you eat?')!

So, what is it that makes our moms' food so special? Scientifically, the chances are high that we have inherited at least some of our enzymes from our parents, so what tastes good to them probably tastes good to us too. Maybe it also has to do with the link between memory and taste.

As Mitch Albom once said, 'I don't know what it is about food your mother makes for you, especially when it's something that anyone can make—pancakes, meatloaf, tuna salad—but it carries a certain taste of memory.'

COCONUT RICE

Ingredients

* 250 gm raw rice (red or white)
* 500 ml coconut milk (for 250 gm of red rice, use half a coconut in 750 gm of water, grind in mixer and squeeze out the milk; for 250 gm of white rice, use half a coconut in 500 gm of water, grind in the mixer and squeeze out the milk.)
* 1 tsp ghee
* 2 tsp fennel powder
* 1 tsp coriander powder
* 1 cup small onions/shallots, chopped
* 1/2 tsp turmeric powder
* Salt to taste

Method

* In a pan, fry the chopped onions in ghee. Reduce the flame and pour the coconut milk into it. Allow it to come to a slow boil.
* Add powdered fennel, coriander and turmeric powder, along with salt and stir this mixture until it is heated.
* Add the washed rice and heat further. Then lower the flame to a minimum.
* The coconut rice is ready to serve when the water in the pan dries up.

EGG CURRY

Ingredients

- 2 sliced onions
- 1 diced tomato
- 2 green chillies
- A handful of coriander leaves
- 4–5 pods chopped garlic
- 1/2-inch piece of ginger, chopped
- 1/2 tsp garam masala powder
- 1 tsp chilli powder
- 1/2 tsp turmeric powder
- Salt to taste

Method

- Boil eggs for 20 minutes.
- Fry the boiled eggs in a little oil in a pan, over a medium flame. Season it with some chilli powder, turmeric powder and salt.
- Remove the eggs from the pan.
- Add some more oil and then add sliced onion, ginger, garlic and green chillies.
- Fry the mix till it turns a golden-brown colour.
- Add diced tomatoes, chilli powder, turmeric powder, garam masala powder, and cook over a medium flame.
- Add the fried eggs into the mix and stir.
- Once the desired consistency of the gravy is achieved, garnish with chopped coriander.

JACKFRUIT SEED PAYASAM

Ingredients

* 125 gm jackfruit seeds
* 300 gm coconut milk
* 400 gm melted jaggery
* 1 tsp ghee
* 10 cashew nuts
* 10 raisins
* 5 cardamoms
* 1/2 tsp cumin seeds
* Water, as required

Method

* Soak the jackfruit seeds in water and pressure cook them until they become soft. Remove their shells.
* Add 1/2 cup water to the cooked seeds and grind them in a food processor to make a coarse paste.
* Mix the melted jaggery with this paste and heat this mixture for 10 minutes on the stove top, stirring frequently.
* Lower the flame to a minimum and add coconut milk to the mix. Stir frequently till it boils and then switch off the stove.
* In a separate pan, fry the cashew nuts and raisins in ghee.
* Pour the prepared payasam mix to it and stir as required.
* Finally, add the powdered cardamom and cumin to the payasam.
* Serve hot.

ACKNOWLEDGEMENTS

This book would never have been possible without the support of all the wonderful friends and family who enthusiastically jumped in to make my dream book come true.

I wish to thank: Chefs extraordinaire Atul Kochhar and Vikas Khanna for nurturing this baby.

Nikhat Hegde Khan, Vidya Balan, Shobha and Smita Tharoor, Onler Karong , Geetu Verma, Gopi Mehta, Manisha Girotra, V.R. Ferose, Amit Talreja, Sambit Bal, Kiran Manral, Neelam Taneja, Mayank and Pimi Pandya, Aishwarya Sushmita, Kiran Parmar and Geeta Balan, for their time and generous support to this book. I am grateful to C.P. Thomas for connecting me to a very special person in this book.

A big thank you to Rohini Iyer and her wonderful team at Raindrop Media for their support to this project.

My brother-in-law, Rajagopal, who moved heaven and earth to get me an interview with a very special person in the book. I am awed by his determination and commitment. Shreenivasan Krishnan for kindly facilitating a crucial interview for this book. My sister, Sangeeta, for her insightful feedback and for editing key chapters in the book. All my books have benefitted from her fine editing skills. My elder sister, Sabita, for giving me Amma's recipes for the book. My husband, Prashant, for his support as I wrote this book during the tough months of the lockdown. And for transcribing some of the interviews for me as I struggled to meet deadlines. My skills in the kitchen improved dramatically after my daughter, Nayantara Thomas, became a pastry chef. Thank you, Nayan, the brainstorming sessions with you helped me conceptualize this book.

My apologies, in advance, if I have inadvertently left out anyone from this list.

My staunchest supporters Milee Ashwarya and Kanishka Gupta for always trusting my instinct with a book project and investing in it. I have many more books to write. We are in this for the long haul!

My thanks to Saloni Mital for her editing and for her patience as I sometimes fell behind on deadlines as this book raced towards the pub date.

And a huge thanks to everybody who surrounded me with love and good vibes during the uncertain times of the lockdown when I wrote this book. I owe you all.

Sudha Menon
July 2021

GLOSSARY

Aloo/batata/urulakazhanga/batata/patata: Potato
Atta: Wholewheat flour
Ajwain: Caraway seeds
Aam ras: Mango puree, usually had during mango season with
    pooris
Adrak: Ginger
Aamchur: Dried mango powder
Baingan/vangi/ringan: Brinjal/aubergine
Baans ki kalli: Bamboo shoot
Badam: Almonds
Bathua: White goosefoot/pigweed
Bangda: Mackerel
Besan: Bengal gram flour
Bhaat: Cooked rice
Bhindi/bhendi: Okra
Bhutta: Corn
Chana dal: Husked Bengal gram
Chawal/chokha: Rice
Cheeni/shakkar: Sugar
Chukunder: Beetroot
Chole: Chickpeas
Dahi/thayir: Curd

Dalchini: Cinnamon
Dalia: Broken/cracked wheat
Dalimbi/val: Field beans
Dhania powder: Coriander powder
Dhingri: Mushroom
Doodhi/lauki: Marrow
Elaichi: Cardamom (Badi elaichi is black cardamom; and chhoti elaichi is the small, green one)
Gaajar: Carrot
Gawar: Cluster beans
Ghee: Clarified butter
Gobhi: Cauliflower
Gosht: Mutton
Gur/gud/gul/vellam: Jaggery
Hari mirch: Green chilli
Haldi: Turmeric
Hing: Asafoetida
Imli/puli/chinch: Tamarind
Jaiphal: Nutmeg
Jeera: Cumin seeds
Kaju: Cashew nut
Kali mirch: Peppercorn
Kala chana: Black chickpeas
Karela: Bitter gourd
Kadi patta: Curry leaf
Kaddu: Red pumpkin
Katal/chakka: Jackfruit
Kasuri methi: Dried fenugreek leaves
Kewra: Aromatic screw pine
Khobra/copra: Dry coconut
Kamal kakdi: Lotus stem
Kishmish: Raisin

Kesar/zafran: Saffron
Khuskhus: Poppy seeds
Kothmir/hara dhaniya: Coriander leaves
Kokum: Indian sour plum
Kheera/kakdi: Cucumber
Kaleji: Liver
Kumbalangya: Ash gourd
Keema: Mince
Lasoon: Garlic
Lassi: Sweetened drink made from curd/yoghurt
Laung: Clove
Machchi: Fish
Maida: Refined flour
Matar: Green peas
Maampoo: Mango blossom
Masoor dal: Dehusked and split orange lentils
Malai: Cream
Makkai: Corn
Maroi: Winter leek
Methi: Fenugreek
Mocha/Kele ka phool: Banana blossom
Mooli: Radish
Moong dal: Split and de-husked green gram dal
Murmura: Puffed rice
Nariyal/Naral: Coconut
Oou: Elephant apple
Palak: Spinach
Paneer: Cottage cheese
Padval: Snake gourd
Pista: Pistachio nuts
Poha: Flaked rice
Pudina: Mint

Pyaaz: Onion
Rajma: Kidney beans
Rai: Mustard seeds
Raungi: Black eyed peas
Sarson ka saag: Mustard greens
Sabudana: Sago
Saunf: Aniseed
Sepu/sua: Dill
Shakkar Kandi: Sweet potato
Shimla Mirch: Capsicum
Sooji/rawa: Semolina
Sevian: Vermicelli
Singhara: Water chestnut
Tamatar: Tomato
Tej patta: Bay leaf
Tel: Oil
Tuvar/arhar dal: Pigeon peas
Til: Sesame
Turai: Ridge gourd
Udid/udad/urad/adad dal: Split and husked black gram
Varan: Cooked tuvar dal with chillies, hing and salt